The Art of *Self-Value*

A Transformative Workbook

By
Dr. Dalia Olshvang

A wise man once told me not just to acquire knowledge but also to apply it. This way I will never lose—I will win experiences and have a good story to tell.

A Word of Thanks

I know better what to wish for, thanks to my parents who showed me in my early life how to send a letter in a bottle across the waves in order to ask for what I want.

At a later stage in my life, thanks to Tom, my son, I learned how to get on the boat and navigate the waves to become the person whom I want to be. I could not do it without the help of my sister Judith and my brother Michael.

In my present life, thanks to Keri, my wife, I enjoy sailing this boat and directing it to beautiful horizons.

My guides blew the wind in my sails. Dorith Raveh, who guided me from day one until level four of 'Hibur le Muda'ut Al,' and gave me all the space I needed to learn at my own pace. Ben Ha'Elohim, Laila Barzeski, whom I am privileged to learn with today, is a precious, one-of-a-kind woman who has changed my life beyond recognition. Laila; myself, and many others have received divine knowledge and frequencies through you, and thanks to you. Thanks to the knowledge you channel, I became the person my soul wanted me to be. This way, I can be in the service of others, so they can become the captains of their own ships.

I want to appreciate coach Stephanie Freeth, Conscious Leadership Group, whom the universe sent me as a wonderful gift just as I created this book.

I want to appreciate all my students. You are great adventurers, willing to leave behind your old sailboats and are now committed to achieving new horizons of success.

A note from Laila herself

'Hibur le Muda'ut Al' is a program that guides the learner on how to correctly conduct all situations in life in a serving way. The knowledge was channeled to ease humanity and facilitate the daily life experiences that mankind faces. Thus, the program enriches understandings that, in turn, help to change misaligned perceptions and habits that compromise the purpose of life. The program provides understanding and tools that are easy to use, create with, and heal ourselves, and others.

I read this book with pleasure; it is fluent, honors, and respects both the knowledge gained in the program and its easy and effective application. This book is not burdensome, but with its lightness, it makes you curious to continue reading. It is light, short, and to the point, so curiosity arises as to what 'Hibur le Muda'ut Al' is. Furthermore, the book is a preparation and an introduction for those who want to learn 'Hibur le Muda'ut Al.'

Love, Laila.

Foreword

Most of the knowledge in this book is not mine, I got it from 'Hibur le Muda'ut Al.' I would like to acknowledge Ben Ha'Elohim—Laila Barzeski—and the knowledge and frequencies she channeled via 'Anu Ha'Elohim,' 'Kreyon,' and 'El Elinos.'

Many books, teachings, readings, and channeled information from ancient civilizations has been made publicly accessible in recent decades. They have brought an expanded awareness and helped many people around the globe. The only place in the world where ancient wisdom has come in the form of breakthrough divine comprehensive tool set is in Israel, channeled by Ben Ha'elohim (see glossary), Laila Barzeski. The teachings named 'Hibur le Muda'ut Al' (or in short. The Program, or Tokhna in Hebrew) are unique, as rather than providing theories or mere knowledge; they also equip humanity with a step-by-step system that acts as an expanded homeopathic treatment to cure the physical, mental, and emotional bodies. Thus, the Tokhna shows people, in a pragmatic way, how to navigate their life into Oneness, and how to do so with ease. The teachings were recorded, transcribed, and put into a series of books, each carrying a unique energetic code and title.

This is the first time that the knowledge about 'Hibur le Muda'ut Al' has been distributed in the English language, but the teachings were never meant to be read solely by Hebrew speakers. The divine knowledge and tool set are meant to serve people and nations around the world, acting as a trans-religion system. The teachings redefine God, Love, Awareness, and many other aspects of our daily life experience and guide us toward a better life through personal Hatmara. The wisdom and teachings the Tokhna impart makes for a hands-on, wonderful, fascinating experience; one that proves to also be useful when applied to our everyday lives.

Note

This publication is designed to provide accurate and authoritative information regarding the subject matter covered. It is sold with the understanding that the author is not replacing medical, psychological, legal, or other professional services. If expert assistance or counseling are needed, the advice of a professional should be sought.

This book doesn't carry the frequencies 'Hibur le Muda'ut Al' incorporates. To learn more about how to benefit from the healing and soothing effect of the frequencies please visit our website: www.soulawakeningco.com.

Glossary

We've used a few spiritual terms in this book that were hard to translate with a straightforward explanation from Hebrew to English, so we kept the Hebrew transliteration and brought here the explanation. For other terms, we kept the English word and have provided an expanded translation below. Please feel free to use this glossary as you go forward with this book in order to ensure you're understanding is fully developed.

Term used in the book	Explanation	Hebrew word	Pronounced as
Ahdut	A connection with the One from free will and mutual agreement.	אחדות	Akh-dout
Ben Ha'Elohim (single) B'nei Ha'Elohim (Plural)	A soul that is, from the beginning, loyal to God.	בן האלוהים	Ben Ha-Eh-Lo-him
Channeling	The ability to transfer content from the power of higher guidance or the Creation to humanity.	תיקשור	Tik-shour
Creation	The entire divine sublimity of forming the creation of the spiritual and material worlds.	בריאה	Bri-aa
Elohim	A superior entity that holds supernatural power and is at one with its qualities. This superior entity has the ability to Create from the void and the	אלוהים	Eh-lo-him

		'nothingness.' It has endless Creative ability from what exists. Thus Elohim carries mighty superpowers in everything He does. The truth exists in his wisdom. All about Him is knowledge and truth. He exists everywhere and impacts all existing things that vibrate and sync accordingly.		
Frequency		The energy conduction of an eternal vibration.	תדר	Te-der
Gilgul		Lifespan from birth until death.	גלגול	Gil-goul
Gilgul Neshama		A transition of a soul from a body that ended the experience into a new body, and so on.	גלגול נשמה	Gil-goul Ne-sha-ma
Hareshima		The entire moral equipment the soul needs to operate in a physical body: name, parents, ethnicity, needs, physical looks, Hozé, date of birth, and death.	הרשימה	Ha-Re-shi-ma
Hatmara		Hatmara is a change of behaviors or perceptions due to knowledge received. It's an intensification of a change that can be positive or negative (the reader understands from the context if it's a negative or a positive change).	התמרה	Ha-t-ma-ra
Hibur le Muda'ut Al		The ability of unification of understandings from the level of the human spirit rather than the level of the logic.	חיבור למודעות על	Hi'bur le Mu-da-out Al
Hozé		The need, and our will, for self-realization or realization with others.	חוזה	Ho-zé

GLOSSARY

Inner Being	The Inner Being represents in purity the soul's intention and guidance through our life. The Inner Being represents an intuitive internal energy in the service of the soul.	האני הפנימי	Ha'ani Ha-pni-mi
Mahut	Importance and essence are needed and exist in everything that lives, in any situation, process, need, and desire.	מהות	Ma-hout
Meyda'im	The knowledge that has the quality of enhancing life.	מיידעים	Mey-Da-eem
New Era	The era of tomorrow, where we have every day and every moment an opportunity to regenerate and change ourselves and our mindsets.	עידן חדש	Ee-dan Ha-dash
Oneness	Connection with the One through free will and mutual agreement.	Ahdut אחדות	Ach-dout
Self	The logic having created a sense of physical value for its own purposes, so it will experience life through the physical body and apply its will without any supervision (of the soul).	העצמי	Ha'-at-smi
Soul Neshama (Single) Neshamot (plural)	A sanctified divine power.	נשמה	Ne-sha-ma
Spirit	A superior spiritual value that connects and bridges between the Soul and the Mind through pure thoughts and elated emotions. The Spirit directs feelings of respect, love, compassion, and grace through spiritual value. The spiritual value knows to crack the	רוח	Ru'-ach

		code of enlightened awareness. When we are awakening and are observing, we are not reactive, and we can bring forward our free choice appropriately.		
	The One	An expression that glorifies the power of Elohim (God) that is found in everything that exists and everything inside of us as human beings.	האחד	Ha'ehad
	Tokhna	Spreading out a structure of knowledge.	תוכנה	To-kh-na

This glossary has been channeled by Laila Barzeski. It was translated by Gal Goldstein and Dalia Olshvang.

Contents

A Word of Thanks..*iii*
A note from Laila herself..*v*
Foreword..*vii*
Note...*ix*
Glossary...*xi*

Introduction..1

Chapter One – The Journey 5
   1. The silent disease 12
   2. "Mirror, mirror on the wall who's the fairest of them all?"............15

Chapter Two – The Beginning of all the Beginnings............................19
   3. How did I find my Inner Being?..22
   4. Revealing and strengthening the Inner Being:.............................25
   5. Your Inner Being speaks..31
   6. What happens if you do not listen to your Inner Being?..............35

Chapter Three – Your 'Neshama's Reshima'..39
   7. The promise and the reality 44
   8. The journey through the lenses of the Neshama 49
   9. Success..52

Chapter Four – Why Are We Here? The Primary Warning 57
   10. New world order..61
   11. Our Oneness and self-value 64

Chapter Five – Rebuilding Your Self-Value..67
   12. Know thyself:..74
   13. A lesson about faith..81

14. "Thou shalt have no other Gods before me." 89
15. Creating internal and external space 93

Chapter Six – The Mahut of Life 97

References 101
What is 'Hibur le Muda'ut Al' all about? 103
About the Author 105

Introduction

You were born to do amazing things. You've known this since you were little. If you are still searching for the key to unlock the level of success and the freedom you want and are capable of in life, then this book is for you. If you're looking for solutions and have tried everything you know but still haven't figured it out yet—I hope this book will help guide you towards expanding your horizons.

How successful you are will depend upon your mindset, as well as the tools, and knowledge you have. In this workbook, I have put together the primary principles of life that I have learnt in 'Hibur le Muda'ut Al', principles that I tried myself. These primary principles are good for any aspect of life—to boost your family life, enhance your business, handle life-changing events, romantic love, and advance your own self-growth. You will read about why we are here, our purpose in life, and how we've lost sight of it. You will understand how you can succeed and how your Neshama is connected to all of this. You don't have to agree with or understand everything, but even if one chapter of this book resonates with you, it'll be fabulous.

After I jumped into the rough waters, swam against the streams, and made it to the other riverbank, I now know how change can be a challenge and which obstacles you may face on your way.

Consider two different approaches when you face a challenge and ask yourself the question: "How or what should I do next?" The first is doing something physical in order to manifest the result you want: considering all the factors, drawing up lists of pros and cons, and seeking the advice of others. There is a time and place for this approach, but sometimes it may not be effective in helping you to face certain challenges. There are situations that carry no easy, obvious, or logical solution. In these circumstances, the challenge requires you to move out of your comfort zone because the way you would normally solve things is no longer sufficient. The contrasting approach is to draw water from the well, so to speak. From this perspective, the assumption is that there is a deep well of wisdom and knowledge within you, and much of what you need is already there, and it is simply a matter of drawing it out.

I now handle any life challenges using the latter approach. I invested my time and energy into acquiring spiritual and pragmatic energy tools and knowledge to master the art of adapting to life's challenges. With the knowledge and skills I've acquired in 'Hibur le Muda'ut Al,' I am better equipped to face dynamic and complex problems with no clear choice and with many moving parts. In this book, I will share with you some of the insights and breakthrough moments that I've experienced with my Inner Being beside me.

In this book, you will discover how to harness the power of *YOUR* Inner Being, change your mindset, and enhance your life. Each chapter gives you inspiring knowledge, powerful questions, and fun facts to keep you on track with your mindset, strengths, and goals.

In addition to stimulating quotes, prompts, and activities, this workbook features affirmations at the end of every chapter that were channeled by Laila Barzeski. They are short yet powerful and are there to help you to stop, to reflect, and to let them soak in. Be careful—you may fall in love with yourself again!

INTRODUCTION

My Inner Being already knows this book I am writing is ready for the outside world, and that people are ready to read it. This is orchestrated at an unseen level, one that I trust. It does not mean that everybody needs to be ready to read the book that I was ready to write, but those who are ready for it will greatly benefit from it.

Our first affirmation channeled by Laila Barzeski is:
"*Your opinions reveal your Inner world.*"

CHAPTER ONE

The Journey

"Our deepest fear is not that we are weak. Our deepest fear is that we are powerful beyond measure. It is our light, not our darkness, that most frightens us." – *A quote from Marianne Williamson.*

People set their path toward changing in two major ways: the first is through raising their awareness, the second is by being triggered by difficulties. For most of us, we change because of the latter. Why and how do life's events teach and change us? Why are most of us only willing to change our ways after it gets hard? What do we need to learn that we do not yet know?

There is a story about the son of a master thief who asked his father to teach him the secrets of the trade. The old thief agreed and took his son to rob a large house that night. While the family slept, he silently led his young apprentice into a room that contained a clothes closet. The father told his son to go into the closet and pick out some clothes. When he did, his father quickly shut the door and locked him in. Then he went back outside, knocked loudly on the front door, thereby waking the family, he then quickly slipped away before anyone saw him. Hours later, his son returned home exhausted. "Father," he cried angrily, "why did you lock me in that closet? If I had not been made desperate by my fear of getting caught, I never would have escaped. It took all my ingenuity to get out!" The old thief smiled and replied, "Son, you have had your first lesson in the art of burglary."

The son of the thief may not embark on a path to spiritual awakening, but in the same way, the experience still taught him something; and for me, I found that my experience was my best teacher. When I began to embark on my spiritual path, I had zero interest in changing myself. I loved my life, my family, and my job. I was looking forward to starting the morning, getting to the office to slay dragons, and anticipating meeting my wife and family when the day was done. I got all the support I needed from my family and colleagues, and I gave back my love and support unconditionally. In general, life was good. On a personal level, I had always been curious about alternative healing and spiritual studies, so I invested in expanding my horizons. Among the courses I took was Reiki, 'Voice of Light' healing, and 'Hibur le Muda'ut Al.' The studies made me feel good, but I perceived it as nothing more than being nice to have them as luxuries. I was not convinced of how it could help me with 'real-life' challenges. I asked Astar Shamir, my teacher for 'Voice of Light', "Why do I need to change? Why is that important?" Astar was surprised by the question and replied: "Say you live on the first floor of a building, and you know that there's a leak on the fourth floor that might get to you—wouldn't you like to know that?" I said, "No. I am fine with sitting on the couch. When and if the leak gets to me, then I will handle it." The leak reached me years later, but it was already a Tsunami wave by that time; I was handling major life-changing events and learned the hard way that raising my awareness is a must-have. With my blood, sweat, and tears, I learnt that it is better not to react when we are already caught up in flurry of waves that are about to smash on the rocks. It is better to be prepared than to be caught up and completely unready. I thought that I could handle the leak as and when it came, but I did not anticipate the magnitude of the wave. Amid my well-going life, I was caught with my pants down, so to speak.

I relocated from Israel to Boston, Massachusetts, with a family of three kids and a wife. Before the move I had a successful career as a CEO and was an appreciated lecturer in an MBA Program. I left my job, family, and friends behind to experience a new country, new culture, and new everything. I was ready to start a new chapter in my life, but soon after the move, I went into a crisis. Neither my CV, experience, network, nor Ph.D. degree were a good fit in this new culture. Everything I built and invested in over the years seemed to be irrelevant. At the same time, my wife and kids had already adjusted to the new circumstances and were happy with their school and work. I was lost. It felt like I was still struggling to learn how to swim in the new ocean, whilst they were already riding the jet skis. I could not find my place, role, or meaning in this new life. I was miserable. Although I had my titles and experience, I felt hollow inside, like a sailboat wandering in a new ocean with no fisherman to direct it.

That was only the beginning of the Tsunami. Not long after the move, my wife declared that she did not want to live with me anymore and wanted to get a divorce. That destroyed me emotionally. My entire body reacted by shaking when she talked about it. I tried to save the relationship as much as I possibly could, hoping that we would adjust to the new place and culture and that all of this would be over soon. I found myself wishing that things between us would improve and get back to where they were before. However, our relationship deteriorated each day. Life became a nightmare. I felt as though that I had zero control over the situation. I felt trapped with no good options to choose from. I was lonely and desperate for love, a warm hug, and an empathetic conversation. I could share my story with no one. I felt guilty and ashamed that I couldn't change the situation and wanted to end all of it. I was convinced that I was useless, meant nothing to no one, and that the world could get along without me.

You may wonder how a woman with a Ph.D. degree and a successful career could feel so miserable. You are right; it does not make sense. The reality was that I was trapped in a vicious cycle. I was completely dependent, financially and legally, on my wife with no support systems around me. Moreover, I was also dependent emotionally on my spouse, who I perceived as the anchor and my source of love and confidence. When she decided to board another ship, my anchor was gone, and I was drowning. Ask if it was a bad thing. Wonder if it was good thing. Who knows?

Trying to find solutions, I devoted myself completely to personal growth, hoping to build myself up from within and in turn save my marriage. I started taking daily yoga classes to enhance my stillness, and avidly practiced mindfulness sessions with wonderful 'Headspace' meditations. On top of that, I educated myself with Buddhist readings and lectures and adopted the Dalai Lama as my personal hero, whose captivity story and the morals that kept him alive resonated with me greatly. Like the Dalai Lama, I started to declare that I did not have a religion, for my only faith is love and compassion. To support that, I got back to studying 'Hibur le Muda'ut Al'—this time, I committed to it more than ever.

Gradually, I noticed that my reactions toward people and situations changed. I stopped being sensitive and reactive to arguments and disagreements. I stopped feeling like I was not good enough or becoming easily offended. Something in me became *stronger*. I decided to speak less and do more, to become a 'warrior of light work' rather than a worrier of words. I applied all the practical energy tools I'd learned in 'Hibur le Muda'ut Al.' Before I would get home, I'd spread the energy beam of Ahdut, so everybody in the house would feel more connected to their highest good and feel like they belonged. Another tool the Tokhna provided me with was the 'Green Cone,' which was purpose-built to transition negative emotions to a more neutral and higher one. The 'Green Cone' energy helped me open my heart chakra and be more like a sun that shines on a rainy day. Thus, anytime I was involved in a tense situation with my wife, I used the 'Green Cone' to send myself and her unconditional love beams. My efforts were fruitful. We argued less. I was calmer and more peaceful. We agreed to come back together and rebuild the marriage, but the agreement collapsed in no time. The miscommunication and gaps were too big. After trying everything I knew, I didn't know what to do next.

Seeking answers to save my unhappy marriage, I consulted with Laila to get her perspective. I wanted to know if there was hope or if maybe this relationship was over. Laila's answer was:

"This marriage has reached its purpose. You revealed your inner light; you are now a free person."

I was not ready to hear this sad news or to end this chapter in my life, but I knew deep down that it was true. Ask if it was a bad thing. Wonder if it was good. Who knows?

After a few years, my wife and I separated, and I moved out of the house. And then Covid-19 happened. The second hit of the Tsunami.

My salary was reduced to half, and the divorce process was far from being complete. I was scared. I was alone for the first time after twenty years of marriage. I concluded that I needed to learn how to be alone and enjoy my own company. I doubled the pace of 'Hibur le Muda'ut Al' studies as I realized their stabilizing effect on me. The frequencies acted as an Advil pill, healing me from the inside. Internalizing that my balance was *everything*—I was focused on being the 'eye of the storm.' I thought I was alone and needed to struggle to survive, but many good people around me showed me kindness and proved to me the exact opposite. One friend used to stop by to see me, show me around my new neighborhood, and share nutritious recipes that were on a budget. Another friend helped me to paint the house and taught me how to use utilities and other electrical American devices that I had no idea how to operate. I found out that the sky did not fall, and my worst fear of being left on the streets did not materialize.

From day to day, with the help of the frequencies, I gently shed more and more of my old thoughts and belief patterns. I felt every day as if heavy stones were lifted from me. In the past, I did not feel I had much to be proud of—I was a master of killing my successes. If I got a compliment, I smiled with embarrassment. If I did a good job, I said, "It's nothing; anyone could have done it." I justified it as humbleness or being shy, but the truth was that I was undervaluing myself and selling myself short. I was looking for it all around me but was reluctant to see and accept my own worth. The louder and more confidently the people around me talked, the more I followed them. I was convinced that they were stronger, better, and more successful. I felt that I was lacking something; that I was not enough.

Understanding that I needed to change my ways, I took the time to upgrade my sailboat to a yacht. The results quickly showed up. I taught myself how to handle finances and make it through challenging times. I made new friends and relationships. I found a second part-time job to tide me over until the Covid-19 spike passed. I also learnt how to fully accept support and help, something I was ashamed to do before. I realized that when I applied the spiritual tools and had the right mindset, things were working out much better for me. I left behind the idea that in order to succeed, I needed to struggle. I stopped swimming with the sharks and started to swim with the dolphins. There are many waves to a Tsunami. During the first wave, I learned that I looked for love in all the wrong places, and the second wave taught me that I did the same when looking for confidence and protection in all the wrong directions.

There is a tale about a Zen master whom a student once asked of him, "What is the most valuable thing in the world?" and the master replied, "The head of a dead cat." "Why is it the most valuable thing in the world?" inquired the student. The master replied, "Because no one can name its price." In the same way, I could not name the price of having valuable spiritual knowledge and a connection with my Inner Being. Nothing was more important to me than raising my spirit and consciousness. With the help of the frequencies, I could preserve my good spirit and high awareness and make it second nature. The circumstances around me did not change too much; the people around me stayed the same—I was the one who was changed. As soon as I changed, so did my reality. I doubled my income, gained meaningful relationships, became a spiritual mentor of 'Hibur le Muda'ut Al,' I became a guest lecturer about spiritual consciousness, and have had the privilege of being in another vocation as a group facilitator in a mental first aid care line.

Learn from the masters – How to kill success

Here is my recipe for how to devalue your own achievements. I practiced it for years and perfected it to mastery. If you want to master this skill too here is how:

1. Work hard to achieve your goals. Once you achieve it do not assume you deserve the results and say: "Everyone can do it."

2. If people thank you or appreciate what you did, do not take their compliment seriously. Just smile nervously and say, "I didn't do anything special" or repeat, "Anyone can do it."

3. Be convinced that you are humble by not giving value to what you do.

4. Practice self-talk like: "I should have done it better," "it's not enough" and move immediately to your next project.

5. Assume that what other people do or think is always better than what you do or have.

Our next affirmation channeled by Laila Barzeski is:
*"Life goes on – with the knowledge you gained
and the experience you earned."*

1. The silent disease

And then it hit me. I realized that I had recovered from a chronic disease. That disease was called 'low self-value.' I call it a disease rather than just something that I felt at times because it affected my life completely from a very early age. It colored many things in my life, from the relationships I chose, to the salary I got, and the friends I had. It affected the things I did, but also the things I chose not to do because of the fear that maybe I was not enough or did not deserve it, or because of what other people may say. Low self-value is an illness because, as with many other illnesses, it begins first with the thoughts and emotions we carry. Our judgmental, negative thoughts and feelings accumulate and escalate over time, and when they gain momentum, we can even see the effects on our physical bodies.

In the beginning, we may experience subtle 'stop signs' like a slight sensitivity in our heart as if it is shrinking. It could also be that you get the occasional, unexplained headaches. Many people solve these symptoms by taking a painkiller, but those signs happen in order to help us pivot and figure out a different route. If we do not listen to our bodies, the problem escalates and could take the form of emotional eating or social anxiety. Research shows that those who are suffering from sadness, helplessness, and other symptoms of depression are almost twenty percent more likely to also have severe gum disease (as show in the study by Nascimento, G. et al, 2018). Dentist, Dr. Maya Schneider (Schneider, 2018), explains how our gums and teeth are affected by our self-judgmental thoughts. Self-criticism reflects our inability to 'taste' the sweet taste of life which may cause cavities and gums regression by trying to fill the void inside with sweetness from the outside. No wonder Coca-Cola's slogan, "Life tastes good", is so popular. It touches upon a deep truth within us.

After doing large amounts of research, Charles Darwin concluded that it is not the strongest that survive but the one that knows how to adjust. Yuval

Noah Harari, an Israeli public intellectual and historian, concluded that the one that survives is not only the one that adjusts to change but the one that knows how to communicate and form strong social connections. Building on that, I gathered for myself and the Universe, and claimed that many people survive life, but the real mastery is to be able to survive life gracefully. I would like to suggest that the strongest people are the people that understand the power of love and compassion. Love is the strongest power on earth. When we do things out of love, we are more flexible, willing, self-controlled and will do harder things than we ever imagined we could. Think about a mother that moves mountains for the sake of her children. Love is the almighty power, and those who love themselves to a degree, with humbleness and care, acknowledge their value and therefore dance the dance of life gracefully.

I always thought that it was only me who suffered from low self-value and that everyone else did not have these issues with themselves. I was surprised to see the statistics. In a survey done among twenty-two-thousand people from twenty-one different western countries (The Body Shop Self-Love Index, 2021), only fifty-three out of one-hundred people, meaning one in two people worldwide, felt more self-doubt than they did self-love. Eighty-five percent of women did not believe they were attractive, and sixty-two percent of women said they did not believe they were intelligent (The Gee Hair and Censuswide, 2021). Sixty-one percent of adults and sixty-six percent of children reported feeling bad about their body image (Body Image survey, UK, 2020). Looking at these shockingly high statistics, especially among women, shows that if there's something you'd like to inspire and encourage your sons and daughters to have then it is a healthy self-value.

My personal belief is that low self-value is the silent root cause of many of the problems we face as a society. When we look at our surroundings, it could be confusing as people may live in different places, have different family set ups, and have different socio-economic states, so on the surface, each life story may look separate—but the root cause of many social problems remains the same. Psychologists claim that most psychological problems—from anxiety and depression, to fear of intimacy or success, to spouse battery, and even child molestation—can be traced back to low self-esteem.

In one of 'Hibur le Muda'ut Al' teachings, students get energy treatment from the Universe to balance and mend their broken self-value. In the treatment, energy is sent from the Universe to fill light into all the places in our body that carry an imprint of past experiences of low self-value or disrespect towards ourselves and our journey. I can only imagine how thousands of people could feel from receiving this healing treatment and embarking on the path of change. By acquiring knowledge and applying self-healing tools, it could transform the lives of millions, in turn enhancing their self-value and lessening their suffering.

Our next affirmation channeled by Laila Barzeski is:
"You can't be truly happy or aligned if you can't see your own value."

2. "Mirror, mirror on the wall who's the fairest of them all?"

Self-value is different from self-confidence, although they are used together seamlessly. Our self-value is our inner confidence, and this is what really dictates our happiness levels. I gained my confidence by working hard towards my achievements. I drew my confidence from my Ph.D. degree, a promotion at work, and being a mother. Self-value is a more inward attribute that, for me, is not related to the things I have done or experienced. It was not about my wins or losses. I was not afraid of failure. I was afraid of rejection and people not loving me. Self-confidence means trusting in how each stage looks so you can run the show. Self-value means trusting the main actor to make the show successful.

From the perspective of Snow White's stepmother, the way the stage was set was everything. The Grimm brothers, the authors of this fantastical fairytale, did not tell us much about the evil queen, and all we know is that the grieving king fell for her beauty and that she had esoteric powers, which she misused as a witch. The evil queen stepped into big shoes as the new queen and was looking to her talking mirror in order to enforce her self-image. Believing that her looks would guarantee her position, the evil queen was consumed by her appearance. The evil queen was so unconfident in her new position that she held onto her external beauty to keep her safe, resulting in her becoming trapped in a villainous loop of jealousy and concerns about aging and losing her position.

Now. imagine if the new queen had a high level of self-value instead of beating herself up and being fearful of not being pretty enough. Instead of looking into the mirror, she would do mirror work. She would wake up in the morning and say: "I love you. I really, really love you. What can I do for you today to make you happy?" and she would listen to what she hears. What if she could have accepted herself as being loveable?

What if the evil queen had been able to get herself a spiritual mentor to guide her in learning how to clean up issues with people before interacting with them—just between her and herself? The guide could have shown her how to say in front of the mirror all kinds of things she would probably have been afraid to say otherwise. The mentor could explain to her that her eyes are the mirrors of her Neshama, and that is why they would never lie. The spiritual mentor would guide her to know that if she looks in the mirror and says, "I love you." and an answer comes back: "Who are you kidding? That can't be true," then she should know that it's only a passing thought, and not give it too much importance. We would, however, be missing a dramatic love story if all that was happening.

Snow White's stepmother was trapped within her own feelings of doubt and anger. Many people are trapped in a vicious circle of thoughts and emotions, unable to make a breakthrough. Many people may want to change, but most people are unwilling to do it. Now read that sentence again and let it sink in.

The Greek philosopher, Plato, explained why change is not always obvious in his famous allegory of The Cave. The Cave describes a group of people who have lived chained to the wall of a cave all their lives. They had only fire to provide some scarce light. One person was able to escape the cave, and then the sunlight hit his eyes, which was painful. He was not used to such a bright light. He was angry and in pain and wanted to get back to what he was accustomed to, but slowly his eyes grew used to the light of the sun. Gradually he could see people and things, and eventually, he was even able to look at the stars and the moon at night until finally, he could look upon the sun itself. The free person thought that the world outside the cave was so much better than the world he experienced in the cave. He pitied his friends who were left in the cave, so he wanted to tell them about his experience and bring them outside and into the sunlight. When the person returned to the cave, his eyes having become accustomed to the sunlight, he found that he was blind upon re-entering the cave, just as he had been when he was first exposed to the sun. The cave people would infer from the returning man's blindness that the journey out of the cave had harmed him and that they should not undertake a similar journey. Plato concluded that the cave people, if they were able, would therefore reach out and kill anyone who attempted to drag them out of the cave.

I once saw a huge billboard advertising a luxury car with the slogan: "Just because you're breathing doesn't mean you're alive." We are all asleep,[1] until we are awakened. Awakening can be rude, but it is often necessary. You were raised upon truths and narratives. You embraced beliefs and storylines about why your life looks the way it does. Sometimes awakening means accepting a different story. The new story may have a toll, which is admitting you were wrong all these years. Nobody likes to be wrong. The adjustment period can be painful while you get used to the new normal. Nobody likes to feel pain. So how can you still escape the 'cave' and get to see the sunlight and bless yourself for the change? How can you begin to understand the nature of illusion?

People who are optimistic see life through rose tinted lenses. People who are pessimists understand life through dark lenses. Being in Oneness means having no lenses at all and experiencing the world as it is. It took me four-hundred-and-forty frequencies to reach this point. You may ask, how can I do it too? I want to take you by the hand and walk you through the story from its beginning.

Our next affirmation channeled by Laila Barzeski is:
"I'm the light, and the light is flowing in me adequately."

---

[1] Being asleep means not raising the state of awareness. Spiritual awakening begins the moment a person rises to a higher state of awareness and can step back and "awake" to their life with a new sense of being in this world.

CHAPTER TWO

The Beginning of all the Beginnings

Many people ask me, "Exactly how do you help people to know what's true and what's not?" I reply that, "I get them to a place where they can't ask any more questions."

The place where you have the 'knowing' is where your Inner Being is. The Inner Being is the voice of your Neshama. Think about it as a hidden treasure. In order to get to the treasure, you need to first move away from obstacles that impede your way. Abraham Hicks describes our innate nature as if it's an empty bottle sinking in the water and when we stop sitting on it, it naturally floats out. Only when we oppress the bottle does it sink. Our true innate nature is light and full of ease, and it naturally rises the moment we stop resisting. When we get to the treasure, it is under a locked safe. We need a key. The key to reaching the Inner Being is by turning our eyes inward—and listening. Our Inner Being is waiting and crying for us to pay attention and unlock it. The moment we learn how to speak in His language, He starts to communicate with us. We must unlock the safe where our Inner Being is, in doing so we will have entered the holiest of holy places, the place that converges to the beginning of all the beginnings, to the source of the absolute truth. The Inner Being knows what your Neshama wants and what path to take.

You may ask, if it is an innate and natural quality to us; how come so few of us experience the impact of our Inner Being? Well, actually, most of us do experience it but not all the time. You get moments of it when you are doing something that you really like. It could be doing something while you are losing track of time when you're cooking, dancing, or playing sports. A skillful basketball player who plays the game well is often described as being in the 'zone' and tuned into his resources. This state is not that different from being in Oneness. The question is not if we have an Inner Being, but how can we use it more skillfully and be more in the 'zone'? They say that we use only a very small part of our brain capacity; imagine the new opportunities that would be opened up for you if you were managing to utilize them more. The animals, by the way, are doing that all the time—they have not given up their awareness of their relationship with the Universe, and they are tuned into the frequency, vibration, and energy of the One.

It is a paradox, because many of us don't believe we are fully equipped and capable of achieving what we want, while we actually do have an innate ability to create thoughts into things. It is an interesting question; why is it that most of us do not use, or are even ignoring, this powerful innate ability to mobilize our willpower and create outcomes? Could it be that we just do not know how? For many years we got used to living at a high pace filled with loud surroundings that mask our inner voice. For years we were taught to listen to what others tell us—parents, teachers, counselors, bosses, even the media. We are given instructions, advice, requests, threats, and commands. The louder the voices are, the more convincing they may have seemed to us. The more the people around us sounding more decisive and knowledgeable, the more likely it is to muffle our inner voice, which is more intuitive and gentler by nature. It can seem easier to please others and avoid conflicts. It may feel less complicated to silence ourselves, and this is what may have paved the way to us not listening and trusting our inner guidance. Ask yourself how many times in your life you had a feeling, a thought that crossed your mind, and you waved it away, just to admit later that you had a gut feeling, but you did not listen to it?

Our next affirmation channeled by Laila Barzeski is:
"I am in the process. I am willing to change."

3. How did I find my Inner Being?

After I moved with my family to the USA, my life changed beyond recognition. After a few months, I was in the depths of despair. I wanted life to stop and change, but it didn't. My home was not a happy home anymore. I was convinced that I had failed in mending the fence. That it was my fault. The only solution to end all of this was to end me. Deep in my heart, I knew I could not go lower than this. Understanding that I had no better alternative but to live, I took myself to the beautiful Andersen Park in Brookline, MA. The little river running between the green trees and the freshly cut grass was relaxing. It was early morning time with no people around me; only birds were chirping. I asked myself a single question:

"Dalia, tell me one thing that you like about yourself?"

I was confident that I would come up with many answers. I listened carefully, but no answer came. I asked the same question again, but nothing was there to echo back to me. It was like a stone running down an empty water well. I looked again inside of me, searching deep, and asked again:

"Dalia, please, just one thing, tell me just one thing that you like about yourself."

I could not find anything. I felt as though I had lost the battle. I was hopeless. After all, how can I live if I cannot find even one thing that I like about myself? I burst into tears. I panted heavily until the sobs subsided. Then I heard something in the background that kept on going without me having any control over it. I listened carefully to my breath. It was steady. Present. Alive. It was a moment of revelation for me. Alright, I said, that is a good starting point—I LIKE MY BREATH!

The breath was my anchor for many of the days ahead. My goal was to get through the day and succeed by just breathing. Taking deep breaths, not shallow ones. My expectations were basic. Take it step by step and breathe before I react or do anything. Every time I was blamed or accused of something, I chose not to react, do, or say anything. It was not because I was avoiding a conflict, but instead to simply not being reactive. Instead, I chose to breathe—I took three deep breaths, connected to myself, and felt the warm presence of my Inner Being. Only then, from this place, would I respond. The people closest to me who were familiar with the 'old' Dalia could not explain the change in me. From troubled woman with a sad face, who was triggered easily, and used to run away from arguments, instead I became quiet and still. Later, I learned in 'Hibur le Muda'ut Al' that our breath is our connection to our Neshama. In Hebrew, the words are even similar—Neshima and Neshama. The corresponding Latin verb for breath is 'spiritus.' This root is the word origin of a fair amount of the English vocabulary, among them is the word inspiration.

I was thirsty to learn and hungry for a new knowledge that would keep me away from trouble and suffering. The frequencies of 'Hibur le Muda'ut Al' were the only place I could find sustainable inner peace. These were the only moments I could feel at 'home.' My Neshama celebrated.

I once read a story about how soldiers were trained and toughened up in ancient times to become fierce warriors. The soldiers were buried for a few days underground in a wooden box. In the beginning, they cried for help and tried to escape, but after endless and fruitless attempts to unlock the box, they became desperate. They were intimidated by the complete darkness and the buzzing sounds around them. After a while, they learned how to endure the cold and the burning hit. They gave up on the need to escape. They were instead focused on their breathing. They succeeded in beating their ego—it was useless in the box. When they were pulled out from underneath, they were calm but not defeated. They were quiet and ready. Their earthly cravings were completely gone. They feared nothing. They knew the lowest place they could go, and they knew they had succeeded in overcoming it. From this moment, they could not be manipulated or threatened as they had now endured the worst of their fears. While reading this story back, I admired these soldiers and secretly wished to gain similar skills and abilities. I should have been more careful about what I wished for!

Our next affirmation channeled by Laila Barzeski is:
*"I'm responsible for my life experiences—I carry
the power of the Creator within me."*

4. Revealing and strengthening the Inner Being:

As Laila explained to us, we are all built of four layers of light: Soul, Spirit, Mind, and the Physical Body. Imagine it as though you are living in a four-story building. If you stay in the basement and never go out, you could spend your entire life believing that the basement is all there is. You may meet other people in the basement who will also be convinced of the same. If you were to leave the basement one day, you would realize that the building also has a rooftop from which the view is completely different.

In the same way, many people are convinced that all that matters is their body and mind and that there is nothing beyond it. It is not wrong to believe so, but it's a limited view that states only what they can see and touch with their physical senses exists. Many are living much like that prisoner who escaped from Plato's The Cave allegory. The more we expand our consciousness, gain knowledge, and develop the spiritual senses, the more we understand that there are more floors to the building than we believed there to be to begin with.

Some people use the term 'old souls,' but we are all old souls, reincarnated over and over for thousands and tens and tens of thousands of years. We've all been in the past rich and poor, female and male, black and white, straight and gay. We've even 'jumped' between different nations and religions, so we were Christians, Jews, and Muslims in the past. Those varied experiences were all for a good reason, as our Neshamot intended to understand how life looks from different perspectives and angles to enhance Oneness between people and nations.

Realizing that my Neshama is eternal and that she was there before I was even born and will continue going after I pass away made me want to learn more about my past life experiences. I wanted to understand the bigger context of why I am with my wife and what my Neshama wishes for. As part of 'Hibur le Muda'ut Al' studies, I learned how to explore my past Gilgulim, not for the sake of curiosity but for the purpose of bringing qualities from the past into my present experiences.

Looking into my past Gilgulim, I found a fascinating mosaic of experiences. I understood that; the same as those tamed soldiers in ancient times, my spouse was the best trainer I could wish for to tame my ego and release my Inner Being. I visualized my first Gilgul with her when we were mother and daughter in ancient Babel. We were very dedicated and connected to each other. This was not the last time we've spent time together. In another lifetime, she was my big brother, and I was 'her' little sister. We were very close, but I was dependent on 'my brother' who wished me to become more independent although I was reluctant to do so. Our journey did not end there. We had another experience together, this time as husband and wife in fifteenth century Spain. I was not a very liberal husband, and I had a habit of controlling her and depriving her of her freedom. In another lifetime, she was a beggar, and I was a rich person who despised her dirty clothes and look and did not help her. You see, we made a long journey together where we did not succeed in changing ourselves and containing each other. As I witnessed our shared history, my heart filled with compassion. I could imagine us sitting up there in the spiritual realm, as Neshamot in our etheric state, planning together how we come down to the physical world and help each other the best we can. We went down again and again and again. Every time it was the same Neshama but with a different 'suit,' name, and role.

Those revelations helped me to understand my unhappy marriage and see how it related to karmic justice. My wife in the present life came to help me become what my Neshama was intending and wishing for. Which is to reveal the qualities of my Inner Being and bring those qualities forward so others could experience them as well. This way, what I show from the outside is equal to what I discovered from the inside, and I live my life no more with masks of fear and disconnection.

Isaiah explained what Karmic justice is in his prophecy (Isaiah 40:4):

> *"Let every valley be raised,*
> *Every hill and mount is made low.*
> *Let the rugged ground become level*
> *And the ridges become plain."*

Karmic justice means that in every place darkness comes in, we need to balance it with light. Dark and light are opposite definitions; in physics, for example, the definition of darkness is lack of light. From this perspective, when we treat ourselves or other people unkindly (with a lack of light), we must balance it at a later time. It is our job to figure out how instead of 'dark' emotions like hate, anger, blame, or guilt, we can work with lighter emotions like love and compassion.

Over time, my spiritual resilience became the source of my material resilience. Equipped with knowledge about the greater context of my life, I exercised my freedom of choice daily. Freedom for me meant choosing how I responded to circumstances and other people around me, rather than automatically reacting when they pushed my 'buttons.' I learned how to regulate my thoughts and emotions and stay balanced no matter what. I felt like the elderly monk in the story where his students were in awe because nothing ever seemed to upset or ruffle him. The students found him a bit unearthly and even frightening. One day they decided to put him to a test. A bunch of them very quietly hid in a dark corner of one of the hallways and waited for the monk to walk by. Within moments, the old man appeared, carrying a cup of hot tea. Just as he passed by, the students all rushed out at him, screaming as loud as they could. But the monk showed no reaction whatsoever. He peacefully made his way to a small table at the end of the hall, gently placed the cup down, and then, leaning against the wall, cried out with shock, "Oww!"

As part of enhancing my balance and understanding that we are all here, in the same boat, learning a personal and collective lesson, while helping each other to grow and expand. I learned how to help people on their journey and heal physical and emotional pain through 'Hibur le Muda'ut Al' healing frequencies. In addition, the frequencies helped me with easing daily life situations. Instead of being influenced by other people's emotional states, I could offer different energy to cool down and balance any situation. In situations where the energy was tense or full of suspicion, I diffused and subsided the room energetically and sent beams of energy to enhance collaboration between people for the highest good. I embraced the energy qualities of 'Gmishut' and 'Ptihut', so that I am in a receiving mode for any solution that the Universe is letting flow towards me. If you were around me, you could not see a lot from the outside, but if you had an internal camera, you would see my Chakras opening and streaming and flowing. Radiating to the Universe: "Here I am."

I did the energy work because I knew that, as much as I have an Inner Being; other people have an Inner Being too. The light in me could 'see' the light in them. From my experience, I could not really influence or help other people if they were not willing to receive help. People whose door is locked could not receive the light and pure energy flowing to them, even if it was good and beneficial to them. The moment they were closed to receiving it, they could not get it even if it knocked on the door of their house.

Looking back, it was not my wife who changed. I was the one who changed. I understood that when we first met, we offered a certain energy to each other that attracted us. Over the years, I changed my mind set and perspective. I was equipped with new knowledge and tools that could potentially help tens of thousands of people. I changed. My wife did not. Our marriage did not last. Ask if it was a bad thing. Wonder if it was good. Who knows?

THE BEGINNING OF ALL THE BEGINNINGS

Remind yourself what you forgot: Grab a pen and list 50 things that you like about yourself. After the first 25 it gets easier!

1.	2.
3.	4.
5.	6.
7.	8.
9.	10.
11.	12.
13.	14.
15.	16.
17.	18.
19.	20.
21.	22.
23.	24.
25.	26.
27.	28.
29.	30.
31.	32.
33.	34.
35.	36.
37.	38.
39.	40.
41.	42.
43.	44.
45.	46.
47.	48.
49.	50.

Our next affirmation channeled by Laila Barzeski is:
*"**Loyalty to the truth, to your Inner Being, creates growth.**"*

5. Your Inner Being speaks

There are not enough words to articulate, in our entire lifetime, the infinite intelligence that we hold. Your consciousness serves as the repository of all your past and present experiences. It holds information about your relationships in relation to everything else in the Universe. Your Inner Being is in this altitude of perspective, for not only seeing you where you are in relationship to the things that are happening now. But it is so much more. It can see everything. From where you are to where you want to be. Everything about you and everything about the ones that may relate to you is known by your Inner Being and their Inner Beings. Your Inner Beings are vibrationally intertwined with each other. That is how infinite it is.

How can a tiny sparkle hold such an infinity? I came across this analogy the Yoga Sutras tell. There was a man whose name was Li that loved to study. Because he has read over ten-thousand volumes, people even called him Li of ten-thousand volumes. Once, he asked a monk: "there is a passage in the sutras which says; 'A mount can be inserted into a mustard seed.' How could such a big mountain fit into a tiny mustard seed?" The master answered, "You are called Li of ten-thousand volumes. How could those ten-thousand volumes fit into a tiny skull?"

In the very first lesson of 'Hibur le Muda'ut Al,' students experience an energetic opening of a direct channel to the vastness of their Inner Being. The frequency that they receive enables them to remove and diffuse energy blocks and listen to the holiest place of all—their inner voice. There are many ways for the Inner Being to communicate with us; one of them is channeling.

For years I assumed that channeling was something unusual, weird, and even dangerous. I learned from Laila, and from others, that channeling is a beneficial and authentic tool that is accessible to each and every one of us. I have never liked the word channeling as it does not describe what I learned to do. I like the way Abraham Hicks put it: "Channeling is a vibrational state of being synced with your vibrational vicinity and the vibration of the Universe. When you are synced with the Universe, you are summoning the energy in a stronger way, and it is queued up to receive words that you want to say." When I channel, I put myself in a place of complete openness and allowing, so that I can receive, hear, and express the frequency that I get. I am not unconscious while channeling; I am completely aware of what is happening around me. I do not flutter my eyes; that only happens in the movies.

As part of my recovery process from low self-value, I started to write a channeling diary where I asked my Inner Being questions about issues I could not solve or that I did not have easy answers for. My Inner Being provided me with a different perspective regarding things I was concerned with. I would like to share with you some of the answers I received, and maybe my questions can shed some light on situations you may be facing too.

I asked: It happens that I attract people who are sensitive and easily offended. What's the reason for that?

My Inner Being answered: Dear child, those people are in service to you so you can improve your resilience and inner balance and reconnect to your inner light. Everyone lives in their own bubble. Those people seek to be close to you, but they do it in an awkward way. You are not like them. You are also looking for closeness and intimacy, but you don't want to emotionally manipulate your way into getting a hold of the person that is with you. You don't need to use those manipulations as you are close to yourself—you have spiritual tools that you use to look inside of yourself and gain insight. When they get offended, they are in service to you, so you can understand your values and return to equanimity while facing changes in your life. Feeling valuable is something that is built from within. Once they get offended, it's an opportunity for you to get back to yourself. There are easy and simple ways to do it. Look with your Third Eye inside of yourself, go through your chakras and let the light spread from the inside out. Through your skin. You are light, Dalia. With all of your Mahut. Blessing is part of your way. You are blessed.

I asked: Why do I feel guilty if I do or say something and they get offended?

My Inner Being answered: There is no Mahut to feel guilty. Dear woman, you can always fix things and bring the clock back in time. The way to do it is to connect to yourself from where you are and move forward. Ask yourself—What did I learn from the experience? Do I have more clarity now? Did I get new insights?

I asked: Sometimes I get hurt; why is that?

My Inner Being answered: Your pain comes to release you from holding onto false beliefs. Give up on how your mind is interpreting situations. Open your spiritual senses, be aware of signs, spread your wings, and let go of the 'earthly' explanations. The Mahut is the light that you carry within—this is your influence and what you bring to the table. That's all that matters.

I asked: I'd like to have more understanding of why people adopt a 'victim mindset.' Was I a victim during my marriage?

My Inner Being answered: Dear beloved Dalia, with a glowing light and happiness in her heart. During your relationship with your ex-wife, you brought care and compassion. You treated her, gave her insights, you saw the light in her. The only button that was pushed and activated in you was that you didn't want to be alone. You carried with you past memories of a scared child trying to survive, a child that needed an adult to protect her. That is a painful place that you are still working on. Please understand that that girl came to help you so you could protect yourself today through the light that you are.

I asked: I'd like to have more guidance about why I'm not accepting that I'm already secured and safe. Something in me finds it hard to truly accept it.

My Inner Being answered: Dear beloved Dalia, you are looking for confidence that you perceive as lost, and you are trying to fill the void. Confidence exists. Nothing has been lost. Everything was whole from the beginning. That was the plan from the beginning—the plan your Neshama and the Universe wanted so you could experience what you needed to experience. You are the one that decided to give power to external things—assuming this will give you more control over things going on. You assume that things will become more secure when you place a cause-and-effect correlation. That's an illusion. What is confidence? Confidence is making decisions according to your values, such as Integrity, Truth, Honesty, Purity, and Humbleness. You should not be afraid or concerned. Confidence is shedding light on things from the perspective of your Inner Being. Once you are One with your Inner Being, that will bring assurance, security, and sureness (All come from the same origin—DO). Trust your Inner Being and its connection to the Creation. In the past, you met people whose egos and control confused you (and made you lose confidence in your inner voice – DO). They wished to confront you with 'facts' because you believed in the truth of the inner light. Be gentle, compassionate, and loving, and know that the truth is within you. Flow with life. If you get an idea or an impulse to do something; follow it, apply it, and so forth. Life will navigate you. Be blessed.

Our next affirmation channeled by Laila Barzeski is:
*"When I'm not in doubt of myself, of who I am and how I came here,
I have integrated energy to serve me in any situation, time and place."*

6. What happens if you do not listen to your Inner Being?

Imagine that you are falling from an airplane, and you forgot to pack your parachute; what should you do then? I can calm you down and say that there's nothing to worry about; just hang on; it'll be over soon. Once a significant amount of momentum is underway, the same as a snowball running down the hill, no amount of positive thinking or effort to stop is going to change the outcome. That's one of the potential results when you are going in the wrong direction and are not attuned to your Inner Being.

Your Inner Being, the voice of your Neshama, is there to guide you. Always. The Inner Being is like a GPS guide that helps you to navigate life. If you doubt it or are disconnected from it, you encounter 'stop signs' on your way, to help you reroute and get back on track again. The signs at the beginning are subtle. You may feel a bit of inconvenience or disharmony in your body, and maybe you cross a thought like: "Maybe I should do things differently." This thought is so subtle that most people disregard it, saying, "It'll be alright!" and continue to act as usual. Then the stop signs escalate. Things may get stuck or not work as you expect. This phase is less subtle and doesn't stay as a thought or a physical sense but, instead, becomes part of your physical reality. It could be that you tried to send an email, and it bounces back, or your internet shuts down. Perhaps a person you are looking for doesn't get back to you. Another potential sign is that people react to you in an unpleasant way or are unwilling to collaborate with you. It could even be that you get a slight injury. Those are all examples of the Inner Being and your guides trying in many ways to get your attention and 'impede' you, so you have another chance to check yourself and see if you are on track. The way they try to grab your attention is by first tickling you, and if you don't listen, you get a nudge, then a slight bump, and if you're really stubborn, then life will punch you in the face.

When we think and say to ourselves things like, "I'm not enough," and devalue ourselves, it's like contradicting the natural law of life. When we are in this circle of thought, we destabilize our roots and stability, throwing ourselves away from balance. We are telling our Inner Being: "I don't believe you exist; I don't believe the Neshama and the Universe exist; I don't think you have value and can shield me from pain. There's no one there for me. I'm alone in this world and need protection and to feel safe, so I'll get it from the outside."

Hillel the Elder (also known as 'Hillel Hazaken') was one of the most influential rabbis in Jewish history. In Pirkei Avot (1:14), the compilation of the ethical teachings of the Rabbinic, he stated:

> *"If I am not for me, who will be for me?*
> *And when I am for myself alone, what am I?*
> *And if not now, then when?"*

Most people translate it as, "I need to be a bit of an egotist and think only about myself; otherwise, who will do it then for me?" But Hillel the Elder doesn't talk about selfishness. Alternatively, he is saying: If I'm not with my Inner Being, so who am I? If I'm separated from my Inner Being, then I'm alone, and when is the best time to connect to my Inner Being, the true me? It is now.

Thoughts have power, and we may be in trouble when negative thoughts gain momentum. Abraham Hicks illustrates this situation with how driving can be on the top of one of San Francisco's hills: "Imagine perching your car at the top of one of those hills and taking it out of gear and taking the parking brake off. And now, just for fun, to see what will happen, you nudge your car a little bit from behind. Well, you know what will happen. With only a slight nudge, your car will go down the hill. But if you step out in front of it right away and let it bump up against you, you can easily stop that unwanted momentum. You would not want to be at the base of that hill trying to stop the momentum." Our mind acts in the same way.

As with the car rolling down a hill, you can be trapped in a 'snowball effect.' Your mind could perceive something that happens as intimidating and compromising your survival and safety. It could even be something that someone said or did that made you uncomfortable. This triggers your thoughts, feelings, and physical reactions. By the time you sense your body reacting, it is already packed with adrenalin, cortisol, and other hormones. Meaning that you are already caught in a loop that has gained momentum and is harder to stop. When you are caught in the snowball effect, you are reacting and, thus, have no freedom to choose. When 'danger' gets in your way, it's already too late because your brain reacts immediately. In this situation, you have zero control over your reactions. You don't have time to process data and overthink stuff, and you react automatically, so that you will survive. That's why it's important to train the mind in peaceful times and 'get ready to be ready.' Being mindful in regular times helps you become familiar with what balance looks and feels like. This way, you can be quicker in identifying that moment your balance is compromised—when the car starts rolling down the hill. This way it's easier to pivot and not get caught in the momentum in the first place.

Before you act upon an issue you want to change in your life ask yourself these questions slowly. Let them sink and see if you answer YES to them or not.

- Am I seeing this issue as a problem and a difficulty or am I willing to place my attention on how this issue is here for my learning?

- Am willing to take this challenge because I can see how my soul navigates me to an experience that I can learn and expand from?

- Am I completely accepting the tradeoffs and the challenges the experience brings?

- Am I happy and curious about what I'll find out from this experience and what it has to teach me?

- Am I willing to take 100% responsibility for my thoughts, emotions, and the way I respond as the issue goes on? Am I willing to stop blaming and criticizing others and myself?

- Act.

- Repeat.

Our next affirmation channeled by Laila Barzeski is:
"Be complete instead of compete. Live in truth instead of in an illusion."

CHAPTER THREE

Your 'Neshama's Reshima'

Ask a typical mother what being a mother is like; she'll tell you that she's a full-time physician, taxi driver, teacher, chef, and therapist. You too, have more than a few identities. If I asked you, who are you? You could say your name, profession, and maybe mention that you're a daughter or a son to your parents, a sister or a brother to your siblings, an employer, a colleague, or an employee. You may also add where you are living. None of these definitions are stable nor do they have a lifetime warranty. Your name can be changed. You can relocate from your town. You can be laid off, retrained, or find another job. The Buddha brought to the world this idea that while everything is changing, we all to experience life, grow, and evolve. We exit this world as souls, leaving behind our skin and bones, and return to our real home, the home of the Neshamot[2]. Without your Neshama, your body cannot exist. Your Neshama is the one that gives your body its power of living. It reminds me of the story of a famous spiritual teacher that came to the front door of the King's palace. None of the guards tried to stop him as he entered and made his way to where the King himself was sitting on his throne.

"What do you want?" asked the King, immediately recognizing the visitor.

"I would like a place to sleep in this inn," replied the teacher.

---

[2] Neshamot is the plural of Neshama: see glossary

"But this is not an inn," said the King, "it is my palace."

"May I ask who owned this palace before you?"

"My father. He is dead."

"And who owned it before him?"

"My grandfather. He too is dead."

"And this place where people live for a short time and then move on; did I hear you say that it is NOT an inn?"

You may think that you are separated from Creation. That you just live your life, and that's all there is. The reality is that you are part of the Universe, and your guides are watching you all the time. Like nature is always evolving and changing, so is the Universe, and as you grow and rise on planet earth, so does the Universe expand. The Creation is evolving with you. Before you can remember, you were born after your Neshama 'signed' an agreement with Creation. This agreement is called the Reshima. The Reshima includes the choices that your Neshama makes so she could experience the life experience she wishes for. In the same way a hiker goes to an outdoor gear shop to get ready for a hiking adventure, so is the Neshama equipping herself with the qualities she believes will support her best while she's wandering on the paths of life. The Neshama, included in the Reshima, everything you are: your genetics, your name, your date of birth and day of exit from this world, who your parents will be, who'll be the partner you marry, your occupation, and so on and so forth. With this 'passport,' your Neshama is leaving the spiritual plane, and comes down to mother earth.

While she's still an etheric figure without a body, the Neshama has complete freedom to choose what experiences she would like to learn and do. This choice depends on her previous life experiences and if they went well. The Neshama would like to experience things that didn't go well in the past so she can learn and fix them. For example, there are Neshamot that choose to learn how to let go of fear and guilt or become more independent. For this reason, the Neshama collaborates with other Neshamot to help her out. Thus, the Reshima helps the soul to execute a Hozé that the Neshama created, to learn lessons she wasn't able to accomplish in her past lives. She 'cuts a deal' with other Neshamot to support her. It gives a whole new meaning to the phrase, "We are all in this together."

It sounds like you have no control or choice over your life, but things are actually in your hands. Your Neshama chooses what you'll experience, with whom, and how you are going to do it with the community around you. This was already pre-ordered and agreed upon. When you start living your life, you are the one who decides HOW you want to run the show. If a Neshama wants to learn how to be independent, she may choose to be born to controlling parents. Why? Because the best way to learn what independence is, is by having a chance to confront control and the limitations over the choice a child can make. During childhood, while experiencing control, the child develops a strong desire for freedom and the ability to choose. The child doesn't know how to handle the situation yet, but as he grows up and is less dependent on his parents, he can choose HOW he handles the limitations he faces. He may choose to continue limiting himself and letting the need for control to rule him or he can choose to confront his parents and know that as a future parent, he will not be the same with his children. That person who experienced a hard childhood will be motivated to search for knowledge that could improve his life. Thus, the difficulties he faces will 'force' him to be curious and ask questions. If that person chooses the transformational path, sooner or later he'll expand his horizons to a larger perspective of spirituality and consciousness-related knowledge. Slowly he'll understand that everything has its purpose and is part of a bigger plan of the Universe. The anger and frustration from his past will transform and wind down. He might understand that his Neshama was created by Elohim and is part of Elohim, and Elohim will never want to hurt himself or his children. He will see how he has the inner strength to move his life forward.

Talking about the Creator and about Neshamot may seem like religious talk. I may use the same biblical terms, but my explanations go beyond religion and are not related to any religion. The bible is a holy book, and the Hebrew language is the language of the Creator but it's not owned by theologians or religious administrations. The bible represents the foundations of law and life, and it was given to the entirety of humanity. When the bible is read through the physical eyes and senses, people may understand it as a group of ancient stories or a kind of a history book. When it's read through our spiritual senses, we find another layer and a whole different perspective.

Think about it—you have innate divine characteristics! You already have all this inside of you! That's an endless goldmine of attributes that you may use as often as you need. Fill your pockets with confidence, self-value, love, balance, purity, freedom, flexibility, compassion, and respect. Your Neshama made it easier for you and already picked up the 'equipment' you need to get through your life experience, in the same way a master-chef chooses ingredients before he prepares a gourmet dinner. The Neshama equipped you with the *Cosmic Keys* you need to open the doors leading to the outcomes she wishes for. Those outcomes are already there and awaiting you. All you need to do is stick to this gold mine and follow the moral qualities you find there.

When you are doubting your own worthiness or not trusting your abilities, you aren't allowing yourself to receive the guidance that is available to you and in turn you prevent yourself from reaching the full potential of your Reshima. It's actually you who's blocking and causing the failure of your own success. You are your worst enemy because you lock the entryway to the precious gold mine with your doubts. Most people, most of the time, are not aware of what thoughts cross their minds, what comes out of their mouths, and what it is that their Neshama really needs. Most people, most of the time, keep on repeating the same beliefs and actions. We were not born to be regurgitating animals, but most people hold beliefs they recycle again and again. They learned it from someone that learned it from someone, that learned it from someone.

There's a story about a spiritual teacher and his disciples that began their evening meditation. The cat who lived in the monastery made such noise that it distracted them. So, the teacher ordered for the cat be tied up during the evening practice. Years later, when the teacher died, the cat continued to be tied up during the meditation session. And when the cat eventually died, another cat was brought to the monastery and tied up. Centuries later, learned descendants of the spiritual teacher wrote to other scholars about the religious significance of tying up a cat for meditation practice.

We didn't come to live life just to survive it. We didn't come to say, "what doesn't kill me makes me stronger." We didn't come to planet earth to place blame and to criticize. We didn't even arrive just to be done with it. We came to experience life's processes and learn how to become part of the One and co-create with it. If it weren't so, our life would be like that of a painter who, instead of mindfully reflecting and enjoying painting, he would just throw some paint on the canvas and say: "I'm done!" This is not how we want to live our life.

Our next affirmation channeled by Laila Barzeski is:
"I'm willing to receive, to contain and to know."

7. The promise and the reality

While expecting us to be born, our parents and community already made clear their plans for us. The timelines usually go as follows: you are born, then you go to school, then you might take a gap year, and then continue on to higher education. A man then marries a woman, and a woman weds a man; you establish a family and live happily ever after. We all have a picture in our mind of how success looks and what an ideal life or couple should be. It usually includes parents, two kids, and a dog. Before you even notice, you are caught up with a mortgage and other commitments. I read this story about a couple that had been married for forty-five years, had raised eleven children, and had been blessed with countless grandchildren. When interviewed by a local newspaper and asked about the secret to raising so many children and staying together all that time, the wife replied, "Many years ago, we made a promise to each other: the first one to leave has to take all the kids."

That couple may have wanted to have this blessed family, and maybe not. We're not sure if someone or even themselves asked them if that's what their Neshama really wanted. Before the Neshama enters the physical body so she can experience life, she swears to keep her Reshima and not forget her strength and light. The Neshama has so many plans to execute, so she promises not to diminish her light even if she encounters dark situations. She is prepared to use the pre-ordered Reshima she creates, and she knows she's equipped with the sacred forces of her Inner Being, the four elements[3], the flame of life, and the gracefulness that Elohim provided her with. The Neshama knows that we come with an innate value from the moment we are born, which is when she enters the physical body. However, something can go wrong along the way, and most of the people, instead of staying with the magnificent Creator within them, keeping their promise and sticking to their Reshima, gradually forget why and for what they came. So many people do

---

[3] The four elements are Fire, Water, Air and Earth, representing our intentions, emotions, thoughts and deeds.

not live in completeness with who they are, and instead experience low self-value and self-image. How can we explain this huge gap of how we are born with innate completeness and yet the rates of low self-value are skyrocketing?

We learn to devalue ourselves from an early age. Many children were educated in traditional education systems that often pretend to know better than them about what they need or want. Most of us learn very fast to become 'good' kids and people pleasers, in turn giving up on ourselves and our needs to obey others. Adults may say to their children: "Well, he's only a kid; what does he understand?" or "Listen to me because I'm more experienced than you are." Children may be told that their choices are childish or silly.

Did you know?

> In Hebrew the word **Youth** comes from the same root as **awakening**. In English, you can break the word and get You-th, so the th is a suffix forming the noun of action, state, or quality of you. In this sense, every age is good for awakening and reconnecting to your eternal truth.

In addition, many adults assume that because children are young, they do not have enough wisdom or knowledge to cope with life's challenges; therefore, they need to be educated and gain skills to overcome life's difficulties; otherwise, they will not be successful adults. Many adults believe that life is 'hard,' when they are not aware of their own Inner Being. Obviously, they cannot be aware of their children's Inner Being. Instead of seeing their children as equal, younger participants in the family that join them on the exciting journey of life, many parents speak to their children in a way they can't listen. They raise their voice and shout: "How many times did I ask you to stop yelling?" On the other extreme, many parents will do anything for their children and try to save them from situations they get involved in, leaving them without a chance to practice their independence.

Wisdom isn't something that's associated with age. The journey begins much before we are born, and that means babies are Neshamot who have just arrived from the spiritual world, so they still remember what they learned and what their Neshama promised. When a baby is born, he holds his fingers as tight as a fist, still preserving and keeping close all the knowledge he has. Children, unlike adults, didn't have enough time to get spoiled and learn what they can't do.

The way adults behave isn't because they have mean intentions. They just learned the same from their parents and educators, who learned it from their parents and educators. This way, they are a 'copy-paste' of the system. We learn from our parents and family how to behave and survival in life. If we are lucky, our parents are aligned to their Inner Being and have awareness, so they can respect our freedom of choice. However, more often than not, we learn from an early age about do's and don'ts and how we should behave if we want to be successful. Starting to gradually rely on what our parents want us to do, we deviate from our Neshama's Reshima.

The average life expectancy in the USA is seventy-four point five years for a man and eighty point two years for a woman[4]; compared to the thousands and thousands of lifetimes our Neshama has experienced, it's a brief moment in the history of our life. Our life on earth will someday end, and our Neshama may not have a chance to accomplish what she promised to do. So what? You may ask, can I still come to the next lifetime and fix it. That's true, you can, but what if you forget your Neshama's promise again? This is the way your *Karma* starts to build up.

As with many other people, I was raised to rely on my mind and logic. Through my academic studies, one of the key things we were taught was how to doubt and use question marks instead of exclamation points. In my personal life, it was easier for me to put my needs and wants aside so others

---

[4] From Worlddate.info

would be happy. I was educated to work hard and not ask for much. I was raised upon the values of not receiving praise and compliments, that deeds matter more than words, so I should stay humble and not draw attention to myself. As a result, I was lost and looking for love and appreciation in all the wrong places without knowing that there was an Inner Being inside of me that I could listen to and trust in. From the perspective of my Inner Being, these places where I was wandering were not a punishment. These experiences helped to shape future-me who will seek to build my self-love and self-value for a sustainable success.

Most sports broadcasts and media outlets support the notion that 'life is hard,' life is a struggle, and a that man of power and money rules reality. Most of us are not aware that the people who produce most of the news, TV shows, and sports broadcasts are driven by profit and ego and are seeking to gain glory and fame. I once saw how a basketball game looked before it underwent professional editing. Usually when we watch the game, the cameras apply many effects, like recording the players from 'beneath' to make them look even taller and 'bigger than life.' We benefit from replays of ball landings from various angles that our eyes cannot naturally catch. We are exposed to the faces of the players and know if they like or despise the other players. It becomes a bit of a drama the producers wish to sell us while in real life, it could look like it's friends who are playing basketball in your backyard. Many of you may have seen how models get complete makeovers to be featured in advertising campaigns, which is now creating a source of anxiety for many young adults, who wish to be like those models. As a result, we start to believe in an illusion and move another step away from our inner voice. Because of the way "reality" is presented to us, we have additional proof for why Elohim, Neshamot, or Inner Being, exists only in Disney movies.

The more we believe that life is a struggle, the more we will struggle. We tend to put shields and walls around us and compete with others to achieve things before they are taken from us. We put a smiley sticker on our faces to hide our true feelings. Being fearful, struggling, and in competition does not allow us to make significant breakthroughs in our quality of life. We may change our profession, replace our husbands and wives, upgrade our cars; but it will still be—forgive me all the dear pigs—the same 'ugly pig.' More often than not, we are limited by ourselves and just like Ken Chesney sings: "scared to live, scared to die, ain't perfect, but we try…"

Did you know?

> **The old origins of health come from the old English hælþ which means "wholeness, a being whole." Being a whole person depends on the level of awareness we have. When we acknowledge and show our talents, our qualities, our inner beauty, inner strength—something that each person has—then change will come. When we become One with our Self and do not allow ego to put spokes in our wheels, then Oneness will strengthen us and bring more ease and fairness to all of humanity.**

Our next affirmation channeled by Laila Barzeski is:
"Life's goal is not about searching for the purpose of life, but it's about creating it!"

8. The journey through the lenses of the Neshama

Before I could even remember myself, my Neshama signed a Hozé. After a few Gilgulim, she failed to keep her promise and overcome the challenges she chose to face, She'd had enough! She was tired of not learning the lesson of how to see her own value. My Neshama was determined in this present life to learn multiple lessons to balance all the previously unsuccessful experiences. She was eager to experience what independence is, to discover her self-value, and acknowledge and value the power of her Inner Being. My Neshama planned all of these. After I realized all these things, I vowed to continue mentoring and sharing with others how they can come to these realizations themselves; and can be empowered through the example of my life story. It's a long and an ambitious to-do-list in a short lifetime.

To make plans work, my Neshama chose companions for the journey to support her. My parents, who shared with me other past lives, were happy to volunteer also this time. My parents educated me from a very young age to be independent, stick to my truth and not fall for what other people say or do. They also directed me towards gaining a higher education, which helped me expand my perspective and strengthen my confidence. As you previously read, when the Neshama is still an etheric figure without a body, she chooses 'Reshima' which includes energy qualities which we call them later on, in the physical body, as 'identities.' My Neshama chose to intersect the identities of a *gay female* who's part of the *Jewish* nation. Each of these attributes has a different energy quality, so let's dig more into it.

Every nation has a role and special attributes. The Jewish people are called 'the chosen people' because they took it upon themselves to spread the word of Elohim among other nations. It's no surprise that the Jewish nation brought the bible to the world and that the bible is written in Hebrew, the language of Elohim.

Females and males have different energy qualities. Females' energy is a containing energy. That is also how a female's body is built—just think about how the womb is nurturing and containing the fetus. Male energy is a giving energy. It doesn't mean that females do not give, or males do not contain, but if a female is messing with her energy and becomes an over-giver or is taking more than a hundred percent of her responsibility, then her natural balance is compromised.

As a person that carries the energy qualities of a Jewish female, my Neshama could better align with her goals, but the plan carried a risk. Having knowledge of my past life experiences, the Neshama already knew with whom she had a business. For too many lifetimes at the crossroads of life, I preferred to give away my light and seek love and confidence from the outside instead of standing up to my promise. Too often, I gave the power to other people and circumstances to control and navigate my life. My comfort zone became staying behind the curtains. To mitigate that, my Neshama chose her a new 'suit' as a gay woman. As a gay, I had the struggle of 'coming out of the closet', standing to my truth, and to not hide anymore. Moreover, through this experience, my Neshama intended that I'd gain the understanding that although we are all different, we are all equal.

My Neshama is a planner. While she was still up there, she figured out everything ahead of time, down to the tiniest detail, so I would not bail out. My Neshama arranged for me to have the opportunity to meet my friends and spouses; to help them too and support them with the lessons that they need to learn. She even targeted a relocation for me to the USA, uprooting me from everything I was familiar with so I could disengage from my comfort zones and build my identity from scratch. You see, I didn't have lots of leeway to escape my Neshama's Reshima.

In reality, things rolled out in such a way that I was drawn to the people I wanted to be with; I fell in love, I wanted to get married, I was curious to relocate and experience different cultures, and so on and so forth. I did not know back then that it was my Neshama's Reshima; I could never imagine that it was all part of a bigger plan to serve my highest good. The path my Neshama chose to take was purpose-built to put such pressure on me that I would be forced to find my spiritual roots again and stop denying them. At that time, the difficulties of 'coming out of the closet' or relocating were so hard that it felt like a punishment. From the perspective of time, the pressure made me start asking questions and begin opening up to the world. I learned that difficulties are there so I can change my mind-set. That my comfort zone exists only because I moved out of it. Living life through the lens of my Inner Being made the concept of success a much more interesting idea than getting a promotion, having a Ph.D. degree, or having enough money in the bank.

Our next affirmation channeled by Laila Barzeski is:
"Life is the sum of moments where you experienced grace."

9. Success

You may think that success is about having a nice car and a big house, and that's what will make you happy, but it's not the job of your car or of your house to make you happy. Spirituality doesn't mean you shouldn't have a roof over your head, but it does say that the more you succeed in changing your mind-set, the less blood, sweat, and tears you will need to apply to get that car, house, or those other things you want in your life. The primary laws of life state that only spiritual Hatmara leads to the desired material outcome. It's the spirit that brings the material and not the other way around; thus, from the moment you are focused on raising your consciousness and regenerating yourself, your reality will change as well; that's why the reality you face reflects the way your mind thinks.

You may say, I know many people that achieved things without spiritual transformation, and they seem to be happy. True, people can work hard or inherit what they have. Other people enforce, control, or manipulate their way into getting things. The result may seem the same but what your Neshama is looking for is progress and how you move up from point A to B to C, in the way you think and feel. When you achieve both the transformation and getting what you want, that's a double win.

Words, letters, and numbers are energy, and how they are constructed can teach us a lot about their meaning and their relation to other words. The Hebrew origins of the word 'success' comes from the words 'pass through' (Li'tzlo'ach). The corresponding word in Latin is 'sub-cedre,' which means '(results) come after.' Thus, Success is not the result. It is a process that ends up with a positive result. So, what is the process that leads to a positive result? Using the laws of Gematria, which is the Hebrew alphanumeric ciphers system, success and change carry the same numeric value, which is seven, wanting to say the internal change you experience influences the degree of your success.

People are usually influenced by what's going on outside of their world when, actually, our thoughts are the ones that create things. Before carpenters build a chair, they first think that there's a need for sitting solutions. Then they draw a plan and only then do they cut the wood. In a way, many things we are witnessing in the present are a product of some thought that someone had in the past. When we let things around us influence our perspective, we are actually allowing past incidents to impact us. This means that you can believe that the amount of money in your bank account affects you, but the truth is that it's the other way around. Your thoughts about abundance and money are materializing into what you see when you log in to your bank account! If you fully comprehend that your thoughts and emotions have power, then you can win any situation. What will be most important for you then is becoming aware, as much as you can be, of what thoughts and emotions you have, so if you are sloppy with your thoughts, reality will bite you less. When you are aware of how you feel, not only do you have a better chance of getting what you want, but you are also transforming yourself. At that moment, your Neshama celebrates! You succeeded in getting both physical and spiritual Hatmara, by changing your mind-set and transforming fear to love, anger into compassion, sadness into happiness, concealing into revealing, or low self-value into self-worth.

Nobody forced the Neshama to come down and experience life. The Neshama wanted to do it. She has the freedom of choice to come down to mother earth as much as she wants and likes to. The Neshama couldn't care less for your 'earthly' needs, like how big your house is or how fast your car is. The Neshama is interested in only two things which are: how much you contained love, and how much you expressed compassion during your time on earth. When the Neshama gets back to the home of the Neshamot, she leaves your body, house, and car behind. The only thing that matters then is if she succeeded in transforming darkness into light.

My friend, colleague, and teacher, Yaffa Agmon, introduced me to the concepts of the 'circle of concerns' and the 'circle of responsibility.' The magic happens when you make the shift from the circle of concerns and engage with the circle of responsibility.

The moment you let go of things that are strange to your true nature, your innate Inner Being kicks in and uplifts you. Only then do you become the Creator that you are. In the life cycle, we miss so many opportunities to learn a lesson and live from love and compassion for ourselves and towards others. Many children do not make the most of their childhood when they are instead looking at adults and wishing to be like them. Grownups are wasting their precious time on planet earth by competing and comparing themselves to others and judging who has more or less than they have. Many are consumed with how they look and dress and if they have a flat enough stomach. Many adults live in *survival* mode while chasing financial stability and a career instead of acknowledging their unique talents and abilities to access and create from their infinite knowledge. No wonder many experience mid-life crises and try to fix them by buying a new house, getting a motorcycle, or replacing their spouses. As older adults, they look back in regret and wish they had more time to do all the things they wanted in their life.

In 'Hibur le Muda'ut Al,' I learned how to harness the wisdom of my Inner Being instead of relying on my rational and logical mind. Think about it as instead of relying only on your boat motor to cross the wavy ocean, you can harness the power of the wind whilst also using the sails. Some people asked me, "What does it get you to invest so much time in listening to the frequencies of 'Hibur le Muda'ut Al'?" My reply was, "It is true; it does take time and patience to connect and listen. However, most people also invest lots of time in other things, like worries, concerns, or shopping, and that does not necessarily lead them to where they want to be. My time investment brings my boat to the desired destination." In the past, it took a lifetime for monks and people who wanted to realize themselves, to get to this place of Oneness. With the frequencies of 'Hibur le Muda'ut Al,' this path can potentially take a fraction of the time.

When people awake and 'escape the cave,' they reveal the voice of their Neshama. They start their journey of Hatmara from being 'people' to becoming 'human beings.' Being a human being means that all your desires and focus are dedicated to getting closer to your innate divinity and acting more and more from the qualities of love and compassion, balance, Mahut and purpose, according to what is true and right, with fairness and freedom and honesty and purity. It may seem 'too much', but these parameters are the characteristics your Neshama already holds.

All of our Neshamot have the same goal, to reach Oneness. We all want to reach the mountain peak so we can breathe fresh air and have the ultimate view. However, there are no shortcuts on the way to the top. On this journey, we may all be in different stations and awareness levels. Some may climb faster than others, and some make their way in circles, but your Neshama has a wish that she strives to accomplish. Until you do not learn the lesson, she will persist in bringing

opportunities. Your Neshama is tremendously excited to outgrow this lesson. She knows she can do it. That's why she joined this journey. From the perspective of the Neshama, she is on a timed vacation on planet earth before she goes back to her real home, the home of the Neshamot. She's ready to experience life. She'd never say: Anyways I'm getting back home, so why bother step out of the door.

WHAT'S YOUR SOUL'S 'RESHIMA'?

> **Reflect on what identities and meaningful experiences you have that your Neshama chose to support her with her mission:**

My name is…	In my childhood, I was…
My eye color…	I fell in love with…
I'm located in the city of…	I'm looking for…
I work in…	My goal in life is…
My friends are…	My values are…
I like to…	My ethnicity is…
My gender is…	My sexual orientation is…
My religion is…	I have the ability to…
My socioeconomic status is…	I am curious about…

Our next affirmation channeled by Laila Barzeski is:
"There's no such thing as failure, only an opportunity to do things again, in a better way."

CHAPTER FOUR

Why Are We Here? The Primary Warning

"In the beginning, God created heavens and earth.
And God said, 'let there be light'."
– *Genesis 1:1, 3.*

In 'Hibur le Muda'ut Al,' I found a source of unadulterated truth. Laila, 'Ben Ha Elohim', channeled us the story of how and why Neshamot came to earth and what their purpose was. The story I'm about to tell you may not be understood by your logic, rational mind, and by your physical senses. I hope that what your eyes can't see, your Neshama can envision. Besides, you may find it much more interesting than the Evolution theory.

The reason I share the story of why we are here, is that it is important not only to learn from the past but also to give you a new context for your daily life experience. With the bigger picture in mind, you can put together the pieces of the jigsaw into a more meaningful framework than the scheme of 'live-love-die.' The sooner you understand that your Neshama came here for a specific purpose of expansion, healing past misdeeds, and helping others with healing their perceptions and behaviors, the more easily you can set yourself free and experience fewer limitations and impediments in your own life. Life is made of puzzle pieces you came to play with. How easily you put the pieces together depends on whether you have the manufacturer's full puzzle view.

Elohim created Neshamot. He breathed his breath upon them and gave them the sacred fire of life. The Neshamot were related to him in the same way children are related to their fathers. As opposed to animals, plants, or still things, the Human Neshamot carried a unique feature of 'Freedom of choice.' One day the Neshamot asked to experience life on planet earth. Neshamot asked for the chance, and they were given it. When astronauts are getting ready for their space travel, they train to adjust to lunar gravity and wear appropriate protective uniforms. The same way the Neshamot got ready for the journey. The Neshama is made of an etheric form, so to exist in a material world, she needed a material shield to protect her and hold her. Elohim created the Neshamot a physical body that was purpose-built to carry the powerful energy of the Neshama. To assist the Neshamot with operating the body and keeping it safe, they were given two chaperones, the 'spirit' and the 'mind,' to help them with maintaining and operating the body, so as to serve the Neshamot's needs. Thus, you see, your birth was organized and planned as a masterpiece by the best divine powers existing in the world of the Neshamot.

They say that man makes plans, and God laughs. This time God was crying. The first-time Neshamot experienced planet earth, they had no comparison, and no experience of what it's like or how it would be. The first group of Neshamot to discover the material plane is called 'the Noble Neshamot.' The Noble Neshamot were in awe of the new sensations it offered. They were the first wave of Neshamot that materialized and entered the vibrational spectrum of matter in the time-space realm of Earth. They experienced such pleasure from 'playing' in the matter field that they projected themselves deeply into it. The Noble Neshamot had powerful divine power, and they breached the trust given to them and misused their powers. They could, for example, transform an ocean into a desert for no good reason, just for the fun of it. They could blend sexes and species. Some tracks of what the Noble Neshamot did can be found in ancient Greek mythology and ancient Egyptian art that show hieroglyphs of semi-human creatures like half human/half bird (Harpy), half human/half horse (Centaur) or half human/half bull (minotaur).

The original plan went wrong. The Noble Neshamot had no way of knowing that as soon as they hardened their thought-forms into matter, they would lose and disconnect from their angelic parts, the Neshama, and the spirit. The Neshama and the spirit are 'broadcasting' in a higher dimension than the mind and the body. The parts could not resonate and collaborate when the Neshama entered the physical body. It was like tuning into eighty FM on the radio while the broadcast was running on one-hundred FM. There was no connection between the commanders and the field. Tragically, the Neshamot became trapped in the body form, and the mind was left alone to maintain and operate the body; without the help and guidance of the Neshama and the spirit, the mind stayed limited in her ability to follow her Reshima.

To get a better perspective on the magnitude of the tragedy, it's good to understand how the physical body was designed. The physical body is meant to carry and be a vessel for the Neshama with the collaborative help of the spirit and the mind. The body was programmed to have seven energy portals (chakras) to use as ports to nurture the Neshama. The ports were built to circulate the pure balanced energy flowing from Creation and provide the Neshama with all the energy needed to accomplish her mission. However, as the Noble Neshamot were cut off from their spiritual parts, they became detached from the Creation and its abundant embrace.

The perceptions and interactions of human Neshamot on planet earth became based on the limited vibrations they could detect through only five vibrational sensors. These five 'senses' could only monitor a very limited frequency band of the full universal vibrational spectrum. The children of the law of the one described in their book, 'The last teachings of Atlantis' how the first wave of Neshamot lost their angelic, pure nature and experienced a 'separate consciousness,' "A new kind of consciousness that is fixed and limited and polarized started to develop and create a hold on the humans. Disconnected from their Oneness awareness and cut off from the energy of the Universe, the Neshamot were stuck with limited and polarized intelligence in a limited material plane." The Human Neshamot forgot their noble attributes, where they came from, and who created them. Instead of being angelic human beings, they became merely people.

When the Neshamot transitioned back to the spiritual world, they were shocked to see what they had done. The crisis was immense. The Noble Neshamot came to experience the material world and promised to live life through their divine light. Light isn't just a term or a word. In the same way as the physical spectrum of white light is made of many colors, so does the light of the Neshama cast an array of parameters. The energy parameters that construct the light of the Neshama are: love and compassion, justice and freedom, purity and honesty. The Noble Neshamot committed to sticking to these values and acting from them with balance, Mahut and purpose of what is the truth and the right that they know. The Noble Neshamot failed to do so and compromised the balance and harmony between the Neshama-spirit-mind and body. This memory of damaging the power of light has burnt into our subconscious and is still carried with us today as a red flag not to misuse our inner divinity power and mess things up again.

Our next affirmation channeled by Laila Barzeski is:
"Don't expect graceful acts from those who lack awareness."

10. New world order

The Neshamot that did not join the first wave of souls are called, in Hebrew, 'B'nei Ha'Elohim.' They are called this because those Neshamot stayed close to Elohim while the Noble Neshamot enthusiastically went down to planet earth. When the Noble Neshamot came back and understood the magnitude of the damage done, they asked for forgiveness, and Elohim, as their creator, forgave them, the same way a father forgives his children. However, things couldn't go back to normal as if nothing had happened, and the way things worked had changed. The Noble Neshamot were not allowed to enter planet earth anymore, and new Neshamot were created.

To be fully prepared for the journey to planet earth, the spirit and the mind, as good soldiers, trained in the cosmic school of the Universe so they could effectively collaborate and follow the Reshima and the Hozé of the Neshama. In addition, Elohim took from the new Neshamot the divine knowledge. Previously, the Noble Neshamot were given divine knowledge on a silver plate and misused it, believing they were almighty like Elohim itself. The idea was that if people will be seeking knowledge to solve problems, rather than having it from the beginning, they will value it more and be more mindful and prudent with it, as they understand its spiritual power and worth. In the 'new agreement' between Elohim and the new Neshamot, the Neshamot promised to get back to mother earth and rectify the damage the Noble Neshamot did.

B'nei Ha'Elohim were aware of the predicament that had befallen the new Neshamot and decided to come to planet earth and help the new Neshamot. B'nei Ha'Elohim didn't join the Noble Neshamot, so they kept their divine knowledge. When they projected themselves into the material plane, they didn't harden into the matter as the first Neshamot did and stayed connected directly to divinity itself. Lifetime after, B'nei Ha'Elohim built a bridge between humanity and divinity so mankind could cope successfully with her challenges. B'nei Ha'Elohim focused on one mission only: helping lost people find their way back home to reconnect to their Neshama-spirit parts and Creation, as their Neshama wished them to do in the first place.

This story of the Neshama trajectory is reflected in the biblical story of the first man and woman on earth, Adam and Eve, that ate the 'forbidden fruit' and betrayed Elohim's trust. Adam and Eve were exiled from the Garden of Eden and were no longer allowed to return. From that moment, they were doomed to live in suffering and pain, and the role of the prophets was to be the messengers of Elohim who taught and guided the people to reconnect with their angelic parts.

B'nei Ha'Elohim are living among us, but they are anonymous, and they themselves are not aware they are B'nei Ha'Elohim, though their contribution to humanity is enormous. The knowledge B'nei Ha'Elohim brings relates to all domains that are the foundations of our society—medicine, mathematics, science, consciousness, electricity, music, arts, and more. Think about the greatest innovators of all times, like Albert Einstein, Nikola Tesla, or Beethoven. All were B'nei Ha'Elohim, gifted with unique talents and capabilities that changed the world at their time. Laila Barzeski, who channels the primary knowledge and frequencies of 'Hibur le Muda'ut Al' is Ben Ha'Elohim of Consciousness. Laila would stay anonymous too, but as she brings the knowledge about consciousness, the understanding about her role and the role of the other B'nei Ha'Elohim is an integrated part of the 'syllabus.' On multiple occasions, Laila came down to earth as Ben Ha'Elohim to serve humanity. First, she was in Atlantis as a leader of a spiritual center. Later she experienced a Gilgul as the prophet Abraham who brought to the world the importance of believing in the 'One,' which we call the 'Monotheism.' Laila also served as the heroic Deborah, the prophet and judge, who was able to hear Elohim's voice and share it with others. In the present life, Laila came again to bring 'Hibur le Muda'ut Al,' a new discipline of Spiritual Awareness, to help humanity transform and connect to its spiritual values, in order to ease its life as the New Era approaches. You may have noticed that mankind experiences a growing rate of challenges and that they are having different hardships than our parents and grandparents had. From a spiritual point of view, the reason for that is that our world is in the midst of an energetic shift towards the New Era while leaving energetically the earthly, materialistic era behind. As with any change and transition, the old is still clashing with the new. While the New Era energies are still shaping and taking place, humanity is facing a growing number of challenges, from increasing rates of life changing events to socio-economic polarization. Without the knowledge brought by B'nei Ha'Elohim it would be harder for humanity to adjust and overcome these lessons.

Our next affirmation channeled by Laila Barzeski is:
"Awareness transforms your ability to start your life."

11. Our Oneness and self-value

Equipped with better understanding and precautions, the second wave of Neshamot entered the material plane. Some Neshamot managed to keep the consciousness of the 'One.' Some Neshamot whose memories were burnt deep with the damage that the Noble Neshamot caused were so afraid to misuse their divine power again that they chose to suppress their light powers to such a degree that it was nearly diminished. Other Neshamot stayed with the One to a degree till they dwelled more and more into the indulgence of the material plane and became lost in it. In their addiction to physical sensations, they disregarded their promises and all the precautions they had taken. Neshamot forming into form matter became matter bound. Their awareness of the One slipped and gradually gave way, again, to the rule of material survival and the control of the mind and body. This separation from the loving energy of Creation and their spiritual parts brought new kinds of emotions that were driven from 'not enough-ness' and survival thinking like greed, envy, lust, cravings, fear, desire, and low self-esteem. Many were seeking answers on how to resolve their suffering while also being subjected to being tossed to and from by the tides of the emotional onslaught. Many ultimately became devoted to running away from pain and seeking pleasure in the physical plane. Very few successfully managed to stay committed to the One. To give perspective on how much the concept of 'happiness' was desired by many but a fortune of the few, try to google how many book titles you'll find to carry the name 'happiness.' The greatest western philosophers researched what 'happiness' is and what can make people and nations happy; from Kierkegaard to Socrates, Mill, and Nietzsche. Humanity is seeking for knowledge, but too few followed the knowledge brought by B'nei Ha'Elohim.

Many myths describe how the Oneness was compromised and how people unsettled the divine order. The myth of the Babel Tower described in the Old Testament shows how people used to live in Oneness before they chose to build themselves a city and a tower with its top in the heavens: And they said, "Come, let's build ourselves a city, and a tower whose top will reach into heaven, and let's make a name for ourselves," (Genesis 11:1-9). Humans began to think they were God themselves and developed excessive pride, dangerous overconfidence, with a combination of arrogance. The ancient Greeks called it 'the sin of *Hubris.*' One of the most famous Greek myths illustrated sin and its punishment through the story of Daedalus and Icarus. Daedalus, a mythical inventor, created wings made of feathers and wax to escape from the island of Crete, where he and his son, Icarus, were held captive by King Minos. Icarus ignored his father's warnings and flew too close to the sun. His wings melted, and he fell into the sea, where he met his end.

The term arrogance comes from the Latin word adrogare, meaning: "To feel that one has a right to demand certain attitudes and behaviors from other people." To arrogate means "To claim or seize without justification." If there's someone to control, you'll find someone who's controlled. Lacking the 'one' consciousness, the same as there were Neshamot who used their powers to control, there were Neshamot that obeyed and surrendered the claims and threats upon them and gave away their power. Sadly, the new Neshamot 'copy-pasted' the Noble Neshamot sin of control and surrender.

Experiencing low self-value is associated with the sin of Control and Surrender. In both cases, we are concealing the power of our inner light, and we are not standing up to the truth of our Neshama. Our Neshama understands that we are all equal beings who came to learn a lesson in life. Our Neshama knows that there's no 'compete,' but only 'complete,' that what matters are the values we stand for and not the titles we collect, and most importantly, that it's in our hands whether our life becomes heaven or hell on earth.

Having low self-value from the perspective of Surrender is as if we are saying: "I'm at the effect of people, circumstances, and conditions. I feel miserable and in pain, and I have no personal power to change it. It's better to accept that life is hard and there's nothing I can do about it. Maybe someone else can fix it for me?" Having low self-value from the 'control' perspective may sound like: "It's the blame of others or myself that things don't work out. My confidence depends on other people to be less and lower than me, so I have to keep them this way."

People that control and hold on to things may seem, in reality, very far from having low self-value. They may talk loudly, demand, threaten and blame, but they can still be broken from the inside, trying to compensate on the outside for what they are lacking on the inside. People who are truly confident in themselves don't need to raise their voice, convince, prove that they are right, or force others to do something. People who are stable and ensured by their own self-value already know that they are in the truth. They are open to accepting different people and other knowledge because it doesn't intimidate their inner knowing.

DID YOU KNOW?

> In Hebrew the root of the word 'people' ('Anashim') is similar to the root of the word meaning 'being in a critical ill condition (Anush). The Latin source of the word people from c. 1300 had the sense of "Some unspecified persons". From late 13 century it was used to describe "common people, masses" as distinguished from the nobility.

Our next affirmation channeled by Laila Barzeski is:
"The key to subside fears is by teaching fear the primary knowledge of life."

CHAPTER FIVE

Rebuilding Your Self-Value

Since our self-value was never lost and has always been there, we can find it if we pivot and change our mind-set. We can do it on any given day, hour, and even in a moment. The only thing we should know while we are making this change is that we are the greatest enemies of ourselves, and if we want to benefit from the qualities of self-value, we want to understand first what we are trying to change. The process of change is not about switching on a button and being done with it, but rather a journey of letting go of things and shedding certain thoughts and beliefs until the only thing that stands still is the truth of who you really are. I once met a successful CEO who was sure deep inside that he was a failure because he did not always meet the expectations of others. I read a confession of a successful model who was convinced she has a flawed body. You can be convinced of many things and believe them to be true, but if your thoughts are negative or disempowering and bring you down, that only means that your mind is working extra hours and it's not your Inner Being who's speaking.

From the perspective of your Inner Being, your value is the treasure that your Neshama carries. Let's play again with Gematria, the Hebrew alphanumeric ciphers, to understand what it means. The word soul—Neshama in Hebrew—has the same numeric value as the corresponding word to Elohim, which equals the number eight. Eight structure (8) is the infinity symbol (∞). Thus, the Neshama is eternal and holds divine attributes. When you recognize that you have a Neshama and appreciate the sublime values she holds, then your self-value naturally rises. However, if you let your mind and logic rule you, you lose the connection to your Neshama, as both are broadcasting on different 'channels." When you solely rely on your logic, you lose track of your true value. I want to be clear that I'm not eliminating the importance of our mind and logic, but the right order of things is that the Inner Being and the spirit, our spiritual parts, are the ones that mobilize the mind and the logic for our service. When this order is compromised, it is as if the cucumber wants to teach the gardener a lesson, and the 'tail wags the dog.'

The moment you decide to put yourself together and connect to your Inner Being, you will find that you are distracted. Suddenly you will become busy, and urgent 'things' will show up to draw your attention away. This is not a coincidence. You logic will do its best to keep and hold its place. The logic, with it's limited point of view, is scared and wants to survive. He doesn't want to fail to protect your wellbeing. For the Self, any change is perceived as a threat. Connecting to your Inner Being brings softness and stillness to your inner space, which is potentially an intimidating trigger to the Self. It is like bringing a new baby into the family. This situation could be exciting, but the older brothers and sisters may not like the idea that the new cute baby now gets all the attention they previously enjoyed from. When you start to elevate your consciousness, the 'Ten second rule' kicks in. The rule states that every time you want to commit to something—like going to the gym or starting to eat healthier—it takes just ten seconds for a thought to rise and convince you why you shouldn't do it. You can come up with thoughts like: "Maybe it's not the right time, I'll do it one day, after X, Y, Z happens…" or "I need to think about it." This is not a coincidence. Your Self will creatively try to convince you in any possible way why this effort isn't worth trying. The same as when you switch on the light in the room and the darkness is immediately gone, from the limited point of view of the Self, who's full of blind spots and is not aware of the almighty power of your Neshama; the Self is convinced that he needs to be more present, so it can protect you; then the excuses of why not to do something start to appear. To overcome the sweet talk of the Self and do what's right for you, as challenging as it may be, you need to be equipped with a strong motivation and the intention to stand the pressure of the Self persuasion.

Another angle that helps us to better understand how you act against your highest good is the 'drama triangle'[5] concept that describes how many of us are trapped in the illusion of survival and "not enoughness". All of us, with no exceptions, are trapped in a 'drama' to a certain degree. The reason we might be caught in a 'drama triangle' is that we are the source of the problem. Because our Neshama transferred to the material plane, which has a 'lower vibration' that is also slower than the spiritual plane; we were separated from our spiritual identity. As a result, instead of being aware of the Oneness and how all humans are equal in the eyes of Elohim, their creator, we were polarized and started to hold onto the mind who is consistently fighting over controlling our behavior and actions.

Our mind is magnificent, and when we are connected and aligned with our spiritual parts, our mind serves us to distinguish between what's right and wrong, to identify thoughts and emotions. It helps us to perceive spiritual knowledge, process it, and apply it to real life. This way, the mind is what helps us to transform knowledge into an experience and gain wisdom. When we are disconnected from our spiritual parts, the astonishing capabilities of our mind are a disservice to us. Then, we hold on to our polarities, convinced that our mind and physical body are the only sources of truth.

A great story that illustrates the gap between the way our logical brain thinks, and the way our intuitive mind works is the tale about Roshi Kapleau, one of the founding fathers of American Zen, who agreed to educate a group of psychoanalysts about Zen. Try to grasp the punch line of the story with

---

[5] The "Drama Triangle" was first introduced by Stephen Karpman in the 60's as a model to describe dysfunctional social interactions. It illustrates a power game that involves three roles: Victim, Hero and Villain. Each role represents a common and ineffective response to a conflict.

your spiritual senses. What is it that your third eye senses? What does your heart understand? What do your senses tell you that is beyond what is printed in black and white?

After being introduced to the group by the director of the analytics institute, Roshi quietly sat down on a cushion placed on the floor. A student entered, prostrated before the master, and then seated himself on another cushion a few feet away, facing his teacher.

"What is Zen?" the student asked. Roshi took a banana, peeled it, and started eating it.

"Is that all? Can't you show me anything else?" the student said,

"Come closer, please," the master replied. The student moved in, and Roshi waved the remaining portion of the banana before the student's face. The student prostrated and left. A second student rose to address the audience.

"Do you all understand?" When there was no response, the Roshi added, "You have just witnessed a first-rate demonstration of Zen.

"Are there any questions?" After a long silence, someone spoke up, "Roshi, I am not satisfied with your demonstration. You have shown us something that I am not sure I understand. It must be possible to TELL us what Zen is." "If you must insist on words," the Roshi replied, "then Zen is an elephant copulating with a flea."

Reading this story with your physical senses may confuse you in the same way the group of psychoanalysts was confused. Reading the story with your spiritual senses may reveal to you the beauty and simplicity of life when we pull away the masks and limitations, we understand the Mahut of life, which is 'tasting' life to its fullest and enjoying its scent and beauty, trying not to leave something 'rotten' behind us... At the end all we leave behind us is our skin and bones; When we are alive, we carry the almighty power of love like Elohim itself, we are powerful as an elephant, but at the same time, we are Nothing, like a flea. When we are disconnected from our spirituality, we can't always be sharp with what we see and sense around us; these things may look simplistic to us.

When we are trapped in the 'Drama Triangle' by default, we see the world through the lenses of our Self and then develop approaches like: "Life is against me" or "If people are not with me, they are against me," or "People are either better than me or less than me—and I'll find evidence to prove it." Can you think of people around you that act like that? With this mindset, we are constantly trying to prove we are better than someone else. This habit of thought consumes us and drains our energy. It's equally hard work to keep those we perceive as less than us, below us.

One day I got a call from a woman in her forties who was looking for advice. She described life as a pain, and she had good reasons to think so. She had just been laid off from her job and constantly fought with her mother. I asked her, "Tell me, what do you think about your former boss and about your mother?" She explained to me that her boss is a *bleep* and her mother is a *bleep* and added that she believes that "the world isn't a safe place" and that she can't trust anybody. It was hard for her to see the line between her belief system and the outcomes she faced. You may ask, can't you see that her life is miserable because she was fired, and she experiences unease with her mother? Well, as you have read in this book so far, you already know that first and foremost, it begins with your thoughts; it's the seed that grows the flower.

Raising your awareness moves you out of the 'Drama Triangle' and allows you to embark on the path of enhancing your self-value. When you gain knowledge and raise your awareness, you reveal the existence of your Inner Being and understand that things can be different. It allows you to believe the sun is out there even if it's rainy. When you change your attitude and stop beaching life, you take full responsibility for your actions, thoughts, and words. When you bring back the power to your hands magic happens. Your thoughts and words have power. They shape your reality because this is how the law of attraction[6] works, and similar things attract each other. When you harness your brain's ability and skillfully use your thoughts and emotions, then the sky for you is the limit.

It's hard to notice how your thoughts create reality because your rational mind perceives situations in a linear direction of 'cause and effect.' Your spiritual mind knows that things are not linear and that there's a buffer between the time you think a thought or say a word and when it becomes a reality: Thank God It's like that! Otherwise, ninety-nine percent of humanity would already be living what they were thinking of. This time buffer is there for a reason. It gives you a chance to pivot and align with your Inner Being and its infinite intelligence and attune your needs and wants. The time buffer also gives an opportunity for other people that are involved to align and act for their highest good. This entire symphony is synced by the Universe to help us learn the lesson and make our visit to planet earth a worthwhile journey!

When you embrace a different perspective and change your attitude to a more positive and optimistic one, you gradually see that it's more valuable to learn and grow than to be right. When you are aligned with your Inner Being, you see that control and security are something you already have. Seeing life from these lenses allows you to move away from limiting comparisons and competitions and start to see everyone—including yourself—as equally valuable.

What a game-changer it is! Think about how life gets simpler when you know that everything you need, you already have. All the answers and solutions you are looking for are out there waiting for you to unlock them.

---

[6] The Law of Attraction is a term coined by Abraham Hicks, it describes how all things, wanted and unwanted, are brought to you by this most powerful Law of the Universe which states- that which is like unto itself, is drawn.

There's no need to compete or struggle for what you need because each and every one of us has our own individual path and destiny.

DISCOVER WHAT VALUE CAN YOU BRING TO THE WORLD

Ask five people that know you to answer the below questions

What are you doing or talking about when I experience you most energized and happy? _____

When I experience you at your best, the exact thing you are doing is: _____
_____

What special skill are you gifted with? _____

The three favorite qualities that I see in you? (Do your best to use one word per quality).

_____

_____

_____

Our next affirmation channeled by Laila Barzeski is:
"Knowledge that you put into practice is an applied wisdom."

12. Know thyself:

"When you are dead, you don't know you are dead, but it is a difficult time for your dear ones. The same goes about stupidity." – Anonymous.

There are things that you know, that you already know. There are things you know that you don't know, and there are unknowns that are unknown. The latter unknowns fall in the range of the critical things you should be aware of because they can appear out of nowhere and 'sting' you when you are unprepared. The 'unknown unknowns' are like the blind spots of a car, where you drive and cannot see when looking into the rearview or side-view mirrors. The fact that you don't see in the mirror that there's a bike rider just beside you, doesn't mean he isn't there. Some of your beliefs, thoughts, and emotions are the 'unknown unknowns' that act as blind spots in your personal life. If you do not check them skillfully, they will stay hidden from you and act as a 'dormant button' that can potentially trigger and manipulate you without you even knowing. How can you be aware of something that is masked and concealed? And what is that something that is hidden?

The reason we are not aware of some of our beliefs is because they communicate with us through subtle signs. Like a detective checking the crime scene for signs and tracks to discover what happened; so, do our beliefs leave tracks behind that are shown in the way we talk, the way we do things, and the results we get. You may ask, why should I ride this wave to reveal my hidden beliefs? Well, many of the beliefs and thoughts that served you in the past are no longer helping you in the present and may even impede your way. In the same way you cannot get to your destination if the road is blocked by police or a fallen tree; you can't achieve the things you want if your thoughts and emotions are contradicting your goals. It's like being that man holding an umbrella tightly in his hands and looking up to the sky, seeking the sun. He expects to see the sun but can't see it, so he becomes aggravated, frustrated, and impatient. The 'umbrella' represents our limiting beliefs and thoughts that mask our reality and hide our 'sun'—our Inner Being from us. It may sound silly that the man is not aware that holding the umbrella tightly keeps the sun hidden from him, but many of us are reacting the same in real life.

They say that the mind is like an iceberg, it floats with only one-seventh of its bulk above water. In order to understand what's really going on you need to dive and look inwards for deep insights. This act of observation is the essence of the 'spiritual' work. Many people think that 'spirituality' is all about getting into a state of 'Nirvana.' That could be a potential result; but if you do it right, you don't want to skip the stage of quietly and respectfully observing and investigating the situation with your Inner Being beside you as you deactivate the 'umbrella.' Only then will you have a better chance of experiencing the sublime feeling associated with the state of 'Nirvana.'

Your sign to know if you are holding an 'umbrella' that is impeding your way is when things are stuck or they don't work out the way you expect them; otherwise, the results you wish for should arrive quite fast. On the surface, it may seem that it's other people or circumstances around you that block your way but when things get stuck or become difficult, it's one of the ways the Universe is signaling you to stop, reflect, and do the spiritual work. The reason it works this way is because similar things energetically align and attract each other. Even if you can't recognize the beliefs that are buried inside, they are still active and triggering you and there's a chance that they are the ones impeding your way.

I learned how this process works in one of my 'Aha!' moments where I noticed the 'umbrella' that was impeding my way towards being given a raise. After a year of hard work and doing the heavy lifting for a number of projects, I asked my boss to increase my salary. My boss agreed and I was grateful and happy for his trust in me. We agreed that I would remind him about the raise before the quarter's end. When the right time came, I emailed him, but there was no response. "He's probably busy; I'll wait," I said to myself, and after a week, I sent another reminder. There was still no response. Nothing. Zero. Complete disregard. I started to get aggravated. I couldn't understand how he could not keep up to his word. It was frustrating. From this place, I reminded myself that I have the knowledge and tools to handle situations such as these. On my lunch break, I went to a nearby grove to calm down from my emotional turbulence. The silence of nature around me slowed me down, and I could take a step back and relax. I took a few deep breaths, which further calmed my entire body. I stopped blaming the boss and the situation and asked myself one single question:

What is it in me that prevents me from getting the raise?

No answer came.

I continued breathing and asked the same question again.

What is it in me that prevents me from getting the raise?

I wasn't expecting an answer, nor did I try to solve anything. I was just curious and open to discovering what was hiding there. And then the answer came. It wasn't a thought. It was an inner voice—an insight—that I was moved by with its authenticity. A voice in me whispered gently: "*You don't deserve it.*" Is that what I really think about myself? If yes, this belief is wrong; I checked with myself again for if there was any other reason I did not deserve the raise, and I understood that it was only my belief that separated me from the promotion. It was my low self-value that told me that I did not deserve it.

I was deeply relieved. I got it. I found my 'umbrella'! I didn't know that I held the belief that, "I do not deserve it." It was masked with blame, anger, and wanting to prove myself above and beyond all else, so I'll not feel the pain of such a wrong assumption. Stopping the blame of the situation removed the 'umbrella' and let a new energy flow in. By meditating and finding inner peace, I entered a place inside of me that was beyond my thoughts and emotions—that place provided me with an authentic answer. After two days, without even mentioning anything to my boss, the raise was approved. This is how spiritual work goes in practice. The more you let go of old beliefs and change your mind-set, the more you cast away darkness and let the sunshine in.

Another angle to the story is that without my boss, I couldn't gain those insights. It's not that he wanted to trigger me on purpose, but his response mirrored what I was 'broadcasting' without me even being aware. On the Neshama level, he was in 'service' to me, although, in reality, it looked like he was not living up to his word. From this experience, I learned to see in any person and situation as *allies*. No matter what, with no exceptions.

Abraham Hicks explains, "This world is made up of allies and collaborative components that interact and create with each other. Things then are not happening by chance or by accident. People may say it's a coincidence, but what they really do—without even noticing it—is create incidents." Everything has a reason in the sense that the same things attract each other, so if you offer a certain energy, you reciprocally attract the same energy back to you. Because your thoughts, emotions, and words are *energy* that acts like a magnet, the moment you think, feel and talk, energy radiates from you the same way a piece of music carries a sound wave. It is not something you can smell, see, touch, or be aware of all the time. You are actually similar to a walking broadcasting TV in which people react to what they sense in you and not necessarily to what you say. Think about a situation where you enter a room full of people, and although all are quiet, you can sense the tension in the room. You may be staying with some people, and though they will be silent, you will feel that something is off. That there is something in yours or their energy that isn't aligning.

The timing of things is a masterful creation. It's hard to conceptualize it with our logical mind, but when you are aligned and connected to your Inner Being, everything is given and received with freedom and joy. There is no one to lead and nowhere to lead. There's no such thing as a future or destiny. You are part of nature, and all things are possible in nature. Everything on your path is meant to be there, but it doesn't mean that you have a path. Your discovering of this path relates to your willingness to intertwine with that broader perspective of your Inner Being. It may sound as though things are out of your control, but It's nothing like that, at all. Everything is in your control because you are the source of those things that are happening to you, for good and for bad.

Your Neshama is your life energy. She never meant you to 'cope' with life's incidents and work hard on them. She didn't mean to come to this world so you would just survive life and become stronger from things that don't kill you. The Neshama chose challenges with the intent to transform them. The challenges came to influence you the same way glass paper smoothes the wood. The Neshama wants you to find the secret of how to lead a life from the edge of your infinite intelligence.

Our next affirmation channeled by Laila Barzeski is:
"When you are ready, then change will come."

We will now look at a sound meditation, jot down my instructions and the try it yourself.

"DO IT YOURSELF" MEDITATION:

> Take a moment to get comfortable, starting with your eyes opened.
> Feel the nice soft focus as you begin with some breaths, breathing in deep with your nose and out through the mouth.
>
> **Wait 30 seconds:**
> With your next outbreath, close the eyes and allow breathing to return to its natural rhythm.
> In and out through the nose...
> You will start to become more aware of the different physical senses.
> The weight of the body, pressing down...
> Feel the contact between your foot and the floor.
> The weight of your hands and the arms, how they are just resting on the legs...
> At the same time take a moment or to just to notice if there are any sounds.
> Just becoming more familiar with your immediate surroundings.
>
> **Wait 10 seconds:**
> And then bring back the attention to your body again.
> You will start to get a sense of how the body feels right now.
> Sense a feeling of heaviness or lightness, of restlessness or stillness...
> And to get a clearer picture; starting off the top of your head.
> Gently scan down towards your toes—building a picture—which parts of the body feel comfortable, relaxed, and which parts feel a bit tense?

Wait 10 seconds:

Take the time to notice where in the body you feel that most clearly.

And as you continue to follow the breath in that way, allow thoughts to come and go…

Allow feelings to come and go.

And then invite yourself to answer the below question:

What is it in me that prevents my success?

Wait 30 seconds:

Don't worry too much about the thoughts – don't feel that you need to answer the question in any way.

Just notice what feeling arises when you ask this question.

Ask the question again.

Wait. Remember to breath. Just notice the feeling that arises.

Our next affirmation channeled by Laila Barzeski is:

"The Creator nurtures the light that my Inner Being is connected to."

13. A lesson about faith

People experience life from the circle of concerns or from the circle of responsibility. If you're caught up in the loop of concerns, then your reality is mainly dominated by fears, complaints, stress, and judgements. In this loop, there's no growth and no change because that loop is dominated only by your mind and body. This loop holds no place for your spiritual parts—the Neshama and the spirit. Your Neshama will never be concerned and will never judge you. Your Neshama knows that everything has its time and place and that everything is a lesson learned, not a punishment.

Both circles act as closed circuits. You can't be in the circle of concern and act at the same time from the circle of responsibility. Shifting to the circle of responsibility means that you understand that you influence the world through the power of your thoughts, emotions, and intentions. Many people confuse responsibility with burden or obligation, but responsibility, from the spiritual perspective, only means being a hundred percent responsible for your innate Inner Being's divinity. This immense power doesn't belong to you; it was gifted to you. Having such a great power within you encourages you to use it with caution and humbleness. The same as surgeons will not rush to use the scalpel and operate on people before they learn the skill; so, do we need to learn, gain knowledge, and practice before we apply the power of our Inner Being.

The forces that control the circle of 'responsibility' are different from the ones that impact the circle of 'concerns.' In the circle of 'responsibility,' you bring back the power to you instead of letting external things impact you. When you take responsibility and acknowledge your Inner Being, you stay connected to the Universe, and your own energy doesn't drift to concerns and taking over-responsibility for other people's feelings.

Relying on the Universe and your Inner Being means that you trust the Universe and let it be the painter that uses you as its brush. Your journey then, is more fruitful because you reach your destination faster, without driving your car while pushing the gas in full power when your gear is in neutral. It doesn't mean you'll feel pleased and satisfied all the time and face no challenges. Pain will still be part of your life, but suffering will be optional. Although there are no shortcuts to accomplishing your Neshama's Reshima, working from the circle of responsibility means that you potentially could finish the lesson your Neshama wishes you to learn in a concise and focused way, like an arrow that flies to its destination, rather than wasting your entire life going in circles and looking for solutions.

So that you can use the full horsepower of your Inner Being, *faith* is a must. Faith isn't necessarily a religious thing. Having faith means internalizing that you came as a Neshama to experience the world through your physical body and acknowledging that you are part of the One. Your self-value is associated with faith. The more you understand that the challenges you face are part of the Neshama's bigger plan to provide you with opportunities to balance your Karma's and help you grow, the more you will have confidence in your ability to handle the situation. Like a good general, the Neshama enters fights only if she knows she can win. Your Neshama knows that she is well-equipped with everything she needs to win the challenge, and she wants you to know and believe that too.

Having faith means that you don't place conditions. Many people say, "If I get that, only then will I be happy," or "Prove to me that Elohim exists, and then I will believe." It doesn't work this way. Most of the things you see around you are something that someone believed and envisioned before they were created. If people didn't have faith, many of the things we know wouldn't exist. Why build buildings and pave roads if we don't believe that the sun will shine tomorrow? The trees in your neighborhood were planted by someone who thought it would be nice to provide shade for people on a hot summer's day. The people who planted those trees envisioned the trees many years ago and may not even be alive to witness the strong and tall trees of today. Those people had faith that the world would still exist, and that life would prosper, so it made sense to plant trees for the future. Faith is the foundation of a healthy society.

There is a story about a religious guy who dreamt about the winning numbers on the lottery. He believed that he could win the jackpot of one million dollars with those numbers. All excited, he ran to his Rabbi and showed him the lottery ticket he had bought that day. After listening to his story, the Rabbi said, "Alright then, I'll buy from you the lottery ticket for one-hundred-thousand dollars." The man agreed to the deal, but then the Rabbi backed off and said: "If you had faith in what you dreamt, you'd not sell me a one-million-dollar ticket for the price of one-hundred-thousand dollars."

Only faith creates conditions. If you don't believe you have an Inner Being, then you will not listen to what he has to tell you. If you don't listen to it, the higher the probability is that you will get stuck. Getting stuck may aggravate you, and then you'll see it as proof that the Inner Being and Creation do not exist—otherwise, they would have already help you out, right? What a loop! The moment you give power to things outside of you and allow them to aggravate you, you are already letting them shadow the light of your Inner Being. When you are blaming and judging, your mind is already fixed on the material bandwidth spectrum, and from this place, you can't see the help provided by your Inner Being, who's operating from the higher bandwidth spectrum.

"Though I walk through the valley of the shadow of death, I will fear no evil for thou art with me;" (Psalms 23:4). Shadows are places that lack light. Sometimes you don't have a choice, and you are forced to be in those dark circumstances. You can be involved in a car accident that you didn't create or find yourself in a global pandemic. When it rains, everybody gets wet. A person that has faith in the Universe and in his Inner Being knows that as long as he has faith, he'll be fine. He knows how the Law of Attraction works and is ensured that the Inner Being will lead him out of trouble and make the 'valley of death' an easier, less frightening journey for him. A person that believes, knows there's no 'bad' in the world, only not 'awake,' and that the Creation is always working out for him. People that are lacking this kind of impeccable and stable faith are in a 'survival mode' and uncertain conditions may throw them out of balance because they embrace a 'slave awareness.'

Being a slave means letting material things be the conditions for your success. People may think, "If I have a job or lose weight or have a family, only then can I enjoy life and be happy." Material things come and go, and they do not last forever. People and circumstances may change. When you rely on material things instead of the anchor of your own Inner Being, you are disconnected from the force of the One. It's not the job of money, our house, or our family to make us happy. When you look for security and protection there, you may be disappointed. Your significant other may deeply love you, but even if they want to, they cannot be with you twenty-four/seven. Disappointed by things around you that do not last forever may result in feeling unsafe and insecure. When you tap into 'survival mode,' you naturally try to control your surroundings to provide you with a sense of stability. You are like a drowning man fighting to grasp anything in his way to keep on floating.

Our thoughts play a key role in helping us to feel secure and stable despite the outside being in a state of constant change. Another 'Aha!' moment for me was realizing how my low self-value syndrome played a role in keeping me 'safe' and 'protected.' I realized that when the "I'm not good enough" thoughts crossed my mind, these low self-value affirmations served the old-me by giving me the <u>illusion</u> that I was in <u>control</u> of what was happening around me in the sense that "If only I could be good enough, then X, Y, Z wouldn't be happening…"

The "If...Then" thoughts are described as a 'reward and punishment' style of thinking which is owned by the Self. The Self holds on to duality and polarities because of its limited view. The moment you are convinced that there's 'love and hate,' 'us and them', you live in polarities and start to lose faith. First, you doubt yourself and your own abilities. When you don't believe in yourself, obviously, you stop believing in the Creation. Many people may ask: "If Elohim is so strong, why won't he help us out?" Elohim will never come down to your physical limits. Elohim doesn't do that, but he encourages you to take steps to get closer to him. Elohim created you with the all-mighty power of love. He wanted you to know that you are the origin of the energy of love. Elohim believed you'd live from your Inner Being and use your divine abilities to accomplish your Neshama's Reshima. That's why the Universe said, "Ask, and it's given," because your Neshama already asked for what she wants, and what she wants is already given. The expectation was that with the power of your faith, you'd reach it. When we live with such faith, we invite balance, ease, and respect into our life. We live with more equanimity, generosity, humbleness, and with the joy of life—because we know we are loved by the Universe.

I gained my confidence in co-creating with the Universe when I eas looking for an apartment to rent after I separated from my ex-wife. It was the April when covid-19 had just begun, the supply of apartments was narrow, and people were not willing to risk themselves and meet with people they were not familiar with. I was overwhelmed with everything I need to handle. I needed to take care of myself, while supporting my son, who faced the falling apart of the family he knew, and work as if "business is usual". Every apartment I saw was not a good fit. One place had mold in the bathroom. Other apartment rent rates were too high. I did not find the proper time to handle the process, so I decided to cut a 'deal' with the Universe. During a walk with my dog, I discussed with the Creation the 'terms.' I shared that there was too much on me right now and that I needed help. I suggested that we work as a team and divide and conquer the job: "Universe, could you please take care of finding a place to rent? I promise that everything else on my to-do list is on me." The very next morning, an email alert popped up in my inbox. Seemed like a three-bedroom apartment in the area I was looking for was available for rent. I called and asked the agent for more details and asked if they have any other apartments on their listings. "Mam," they said, "you are speaking with the owners; I'm not a realtor," at that moment, I just knew that this apartment was sent to me through the Creation. The next day I signed the rent agreement after getting a courteous and generous discount. It was worth cutting a deal with the Universe!

Faith means that you know that you and Elohim are One. Faith, like love, is unconditional and without exaggeration, it's the most important foundation of life itself. You don't want to doubt faith because then you throw yourself out of balance and destabilize the Mahut of your existence. Any place that brings you closer to the circle of concerns is not a place where you want to be.

It reminded me of this story I heard about a Rabbi that argued with God. It happened that that Rabbi and a school bus driver both passed away simultaneously and entered heaven together. Elohim welcomed in both of them and took them to a place overlooking a serene valley with beautiful soft rolling hills just beyond.

To the Rabbi, Elohim said, "My son, do you see that little cottage with the white gate and all the flowers down there in the valley? The one over there just beyond the creek?" The Rabbi said he did. Elohim then told him that this was now his heavenly home and that this was where he would be spending eternity.

Elohim then turned to the school bus driver and said, "My son, do you see that big stately mansion up there in the hills? The one just to the right of the waterfall where the golden path leads up to it?" The bus driver said he did. Elohim then told him that this was now his heavenly home and that this was where he would be spending eternity.

With this, the Rabbi turned to Elohim and, with amazement, exclaimed that there must be some mistake. "I have been your loyal servant all of my life." He went on to explain to Elohim that he was truly a man of Elohim. The rabbi said, "Elohim, I followed all of the commandments, even to the finest nuances. I never missed a daily prayer. I learned your holy Torah day and night just as you commanded. How can it be that I am to spend eternity in this small cottage when the school bus driver gets the mansion in the hills?"

Elohim replied, "My son, it is true that you have been my loyal servant. And both of you have been in a position to influence my children. However, while you gave your sermons, my children slept. It was while he was driving that they prayed!"

I once met a man from an orthodox family who became secular. He asked me if I had faith, and I said, "Yes, I do." "Then," he replied, "you are a weak person." Meaning to say that many religious people rely on Elohim, a Rabbi, or a priest to run their life in the sense of: "I'll follow everything you say." This is not faith; this is being a rope doll. The faith I am speaking of is following the voice of the Neshama, reflecting, and understanding what she wants and only then follow it. The faith I'm talking about is believing without a religion. It's the understanding that you have divinity inside and you are co-creating with Elohim. Following the voice of your Inner Being means hopping on the circle of responsibility. When you are living in that circle, you experience true freedom because even if you can't change reality, you can still choose how to respond to it. From this circle, you know that in the same way you have an Inner Being, so do others; thus, nobody is 'miserable' or 'poor.' Everybody has a designated path and journey to experience, and if they are open to it, they don't lose the life-lesson through which they will eventually grow.

I am not sure if a religious person who read these lines would still feel at ease and calm.

Stop praying; start deliberately asking.

Pure intention has divine power. They say that with a bold intention you can overcome any obstacle. Here is how to do it right:

- Rise your awareness and pay attention to your thoughts and feelings.

- Be specific and accurate with what you are asking for.

- Make sure that your intention is pure—the results you are seeking need to advance not only you but also the higher good of others.

- Stop saying: "I wish this will happen." The universe understands only present time. Say instead: "I ask that what I want to become happens for what's good and right to be contained, to serve me and others."

- Launch your thought and then let it go and forget about it. Let Creation help you.

Our next affirmation channeled by Laila Barzeski is:
"You can overcome any situation with no worries when you know that the One is with you."

14. "Thou shalt have no other Gods before me."

The Ten Commandments were given to all of humanity, not only to the Jewish people. As with many things in the bible, the Ten Commandments also carry ciphers that act as reminders for people on how to live life gracefully, from the circle of responsibility rather than the circle of concerns. So that you live life peacefully, the Ten Commandments begin with a reminder: "I'm the Lord, your God." From the Neshamas' point of view, she doesn't need this reminder; she already knows that you have a little Elohim inside of you, but your Self is the one that needs this reminder! Your mind and body are so busy with controlling and regulating themselves that they need to hear: "Hey, mind, hello brain, I'm the Neshama, I'm your lord, your God." The Neshama isn't patronizing them; she is just reminding them of the agreement they had before she entered the physical body: "I am the Neshama, I'm connected to the full bandwidth of the Universe, I have the full jigsaw map. You—mind and logic— agreed to collaborate with me. You have a limited view and bandwidth, so listen to me, your Neshama, because I am the one that carries the almighty divinity. Don't put cogs in my wheels because I know how to guide you towards where you want to be. Don't ask for proof of my existence; I'm the lord your God; please let go and believe in that; don't put conditions."

Building on that, the second commandment: "Thou shalt have no other Gods before me," states that if you have this divinity inside, then why should you be listening to other Gods? Your other Gods come in the shape of fear, ego, hate, jealousy, cynicism, disrespect, pity, contempt, and other 'low' emotions. Too many people's feelings of satisfaction are dependent on outside factors like gaining approval and being loved by others or having control over things outside of them. They worship other Gods like money and material success more than their values and a conscious approach. When people give more value and weight to what others say or think, or to how others perceive them, rather than believing their inner voice, they become *trapped* in the 'concerns' loop and start to work with other Gods. In this sense, having other

Gods means devaluing and demeaning your own divinity. This is the root cause of the skyrocketing low self-value spreading in western societies.

For many years I worked with other Gods. The God that managed me was the 'fear of losing love.' For this reason, the old-me put her own needs and wants away and overcompensated by trying to please others to ensure she had a hold on love and that nothing would scare off that love. It worked most of the time and even looked like it had benefits. I succeeded in avoiding conflicts, angry feelings, and criticism, and it seemed like things were going smoothly. I was perceived as a 'flexible,' easy-going person; someone easy to get along with. It was easy for me and everyone else, but the tradeoff was that I put away my own identity and merged into other people's wants and needs. I was convinced that other people were smarter, stronger, and cleverer than I was. I made them my gods and gave them this power so I could feel protected and safe.

One day I asked Laila what stands between me and my complete freedom and happiness, and she replied:

"You still have fears, and you let other people nurture you with fears. You are the one that gives them this power."

This 'arrangement' that I made worked for a while, until it collapsed. I couldn't fool all the people all the time. My recovery from 'low self-value' began when I let go of my other God of the belief that 'love can go away.'

I've learned that spiritual maturity means that whatever I can't gain from the outside—like love, confidence, and abundance—I can nurture and create from the inside. If I felt that I was lacking love—I could become love. If I wasn't valued, I could seek my own value. One of the frequencies incorporated in 'Hibur le Muda'ut Al,' is healing fear and diffusing it from our mental and physical body. 'Anu Ha'Elohim' even explained to us how mankind invented fear to serve them and that it is not a term that exists in the lexicon of the

Creation. While listening for hours to this healing frequency, my hold on my fears started to diffuse and deactivate.

The Meyda'im include various frequencies, each dedicated to a specific topic. It's like a harpist playing the harp with a span of chords to create soothing, relaxing, and attuned sounds. Contained with massive light and unconditional loving energies; I energetically 'body washed' myself daily until I truly loved myself and rewired myself completely. I understood that it was not the job of anyone to love me. The job of other people is to love themselves, and that is time-consuming enough. It was my responsibility to love myself, which means that loving me is treating myself in the same way I would treat my best friend—with compassion and respect. With no judgment or criticism.

If people around me could say something nasty or disrespectful, I put the work into it—I understood that their words didn't come to hurt me but instead may reflect a facet in me that believes I'm not fully respecting myself. To deactivate and clean this hidden button so it wouldn't continue to activate me in the future, I had to get to the root cause of it. I listened to the related frequencies and Meyda'im about 'Respect' and 'Oneness' that were purpose-built to handle these kinds of situations. While doing that, I gained further insights, and I also treated the people I was in touch with, so they could raise their low emotions as well. Not until I could see my own value was I able to be truly happy.

Practice and learn:

> Start to put value into things you do, nothing is too small to count. Everything that you put energy in has a value: your smile, your thoughts, listening to others, your attention, your presence.

Our next affirmation channeled by Laila Barzeski is:
"I'm in the knowing and in the flowing that the Creative force exists within me."

15. Creating internal and external space

Valuing yourself is not something you can buy or find outside of yourself, in the same way you can't buy sustainable love, happiness, or security. Finding your self-value is an artwork, the same as a sculptor carving the substance to create a sculpture. Many people get upset about why others do not value or treat them respectfully, but they can't expect others to value them if they do not value themselves; it's almost like searching for value and respect from others to fill the void inside. If the way others treat you bothers you, it's a sign that they pushed a button, and if that happens, it's an opportunity for you to ask yourself, "In what way am I not valuing myself? How does disrespect live inside of me?" It's your job to look inwards for better insights. The human eyes are engineered to look outwards, so your instinctive response is to seek value and respect from outside of you. It takes intention, skill, knowledge, and courage to turn your eyes inwards and check what's living inside of you.

The Buddhist metaphor of the *blue sky* can shed some light on the nature of your inner divinity. The clouds may hide the sunshine, but although you can't see it, you know that the sunshine is always there. In the same way, your divinity and self-value have always been there; you just need to move away from the 'clouds' and reveal your self-value, which has always been there but was masked by clouds. There's a story about a disciple who joined a monastery named Kaaksi. The master asked him to go around the world, so he began his travels. In one city, a student from another monastery met him and asked:

"Where are you coming from?"

"I am coming from the Kaaksi monastery."

"What did you learn in that monastery?"

"There was nothing there that I did not already have before joining Kaaksi."

"Then why did you go there?"

"If I had not gone there, how would I have known that there was nothing there that I did not have before?"

Living the Mahut of life starts with understanding the value of life. Grasping the value of life depends on how elevated your awareness is. The basic definition of being aware, which you can apply immediately, is to pay attention to what you're doing when you're doing things. When you read this book, be aware that you are reading it. If you are sitting, be aware that you are sitting. The more you practice being mindful of things, the more it will become second nature to you. The more you become an observer of your life and turn your eyes inwards, the more you increase your awareness. You will be surprised by the authentic insights you can get. Reflecting is something natural to us, and everyone is capable of doing it, but it requires practice and intention. It's not obvious to stop everything we are caught up with; pause and take a step back.

To be an observer of your own inside world, you want to do it right and act from the circle of responsibility—be clear about your intentions, own your thoughts and emotions, and don't be consumed by them, feel relaxed and at ease, have no expectations whatsoever from the process, and be open and in a receiving mode to accept any answer or physical sense that may arise. This is a great place to be, but the transition from the outside world to the inner world could be challenging, and you may want to get professional guidance until you learn how to do it yourself. Letting go of things you are used to holding on to can be a hard thing but a very rewarding process.

When you get to your inside world and reflect on a subject that bothers you, more often than not, you'll find that reality resonates with things you have not yet resolved between you and yourself. Your Neshama, who seeks change and Hatmara, keeps on bringing you challenges you didn't cope well with previously. That's why the most important relationship you have is between you and yourself. The more you know yourself and can candidly see what your role is in a situation, the less you need people and outside circumstances to help you change your perspective. Remember, people can change in two ways, by raising their awareness or by experiencing difficulties. So, by raising your awareness and handling things 'in-house' instead of projecting them on others, you are proactively preventing future difficulties by reducing drama in your life and not risking significant relationships.

How does reflection help you? Looking inwards is a focused and quiet experience where you face and observe things inside of you without running away from your responsibility by projecting it onto others. When you do it right, you raise your awareness and find new insights and understandings about what is really going on inside of you. This way, you are shortening the process and bringing ease to your life because you're getting closer to making the change your Neshama wishes you to make. Reflection is a preventive step, but it doesn't mean you'll not experience any difficulties during the process; as you catch the snowball at the beginning of its fall, the difficulties you face will be fewer. The 'toll' you may pay during the process is taking the risk of feeling emotional pain or hard feelings. Some say that emotions are Energy in Motion, so those emotions are waiting for you to unlock them and get released. They have been waiting there for you and if you find enough courage to go beyond the point of pain and blame, you'll feel relieved, as if a heavy stone has been lifted from your chest. This is the process of 'removing' the clouds so the sun can get in.

Our next affirmation channeled by Laila Barzeski is:
"There are no boundaries, only a need to hold onto limitations."

CHAPTER SIX

The Mahut of Life

Acting from the circle of responsibility is the first steppingstone to mastering your life, but it doesn't end there. From the moment you raise your awareness and change your approach to life, you are getting on the right track towards being a Creator of your life. Life becomes more balanced and seems less and less full of 'have-to's,' burdens, and a lack of purpose. Also, you are less dependent on fleeting moments of pleasure like eating ice cream or taking a vacation. From this place of taking one-hundred percent responsibility, you understand how you offered a certain vibration that created the imbalance and disharmony in your life—it's not necessarily that other people or circumstances change—so you feel good. Sometimes, the change in yourself alone can be enough to do the work. When you are raised to a Creator's consciousness, you can witness your benefitting influence on others, and life then becomes a very interesting place to live in.

The quantic jump happens when you dare to live in Oneness with all of your four parts, Neshama, Spirit, Mind, Body as a whole. This is a completely different phase of quality of life. If, by now, you were navigating your way with a yacht, now you're doing the same with a spaceship. At this stage, you know that life is abundant and that things in life are energy and not just a 'thing.' You stop measuring your success by money or results and live in the 'here and the now,' while also relaxing into joy. You learn how to receive things with no effort, by being mindful, listening, and by leveraging your metaphysical senses, which are synced to everything the Universe has to offer. In this place, you are inspired by the Inner Being that mobilizes you to the 'next thing,' and the world becomes a reflection of your beauty. Your inner beauty has always been there, but it was covered with walls and masks. As you learn how to bypass them, you are reconnected to the sources of your angelic nature.

Being in Oneness means that you are becoming the *source* of things while adapting the qualities of the Creator. In this phase, being in One and finding your life purpose are the same. Being a Creator, you learn how to 'fold' time and create new opportunities for yourself. Since the Neshama is eternal, the only time she knows of is now. That's why the present is a present. The now converges the past, the present, and the future into one point of creation. As creators, you learn how to access your *past, which lies* in *your* subconsciousness[7] and use the qualities you find there to create your *present* while opening *future* opportunities ahead of you. You are where the past, present and future converge, so in this sense, there's no such thing as fate or future; it's you who is creating it.

I was fortunate to walk the path that leads to Oneness. The key thing in this process is awakening the Inner Being while educating the Self to collaborate and listen to what the Inner Being has to say.

Raising your awareness and acquiring spiritual knowledge is a proactive step that is not meant to benefit your Inner Being. He already knows what Oneness is. The Self is the one that needs to be educated. The Self put roots down for thousands and thousands of years and left a deep mark on us in the shape of beliefs and patterns. It takes time to unroot our habits. It took me five years and over four hundred and forty frequencies and teaching sessions of 'Hibur le Muda'ut Al' to gradually diffuse the influence of the Self and deactivate its strong hold on me. The more I learned and got closer to my inner light, the more the Self strengthened its hold on me. I knew that when I

---

[7] Your subconscious holds all the memories and qualities you gained from your past reincarnations.

sensed fear or resistance, it only meant that it was the last dying throb of the Self, so I was more determined not to give up. I learned to love and appreciate the gifts my Self brought to my life. I acknowledged its efforts to look after me and protect me for so many years, but now I have better, more effective tools to do the same.

I eventually was convinced that it's better not to resist and put obstacles in the way of the Inner Being. Over time, the more I was in One, the Self witnessed enough proof of how life can be easier and smoother when the Inner Being is leading. My Self learned how to listen! Oh, at last, there is Oneness between all four layers of light—Soul, Spirit, Mind, and Body.

When your Neshama leaves this world, the only thing she cares about is how much love you were able to contain and how much compassion you were able to express. The moment you are willing to let go of being right and stop running away from pain, then the magic happens. The definition of magic is: things that people don't yet know how to explain. The magic can be explained when you give space to your inner light to shine and move away from the darkness. When you transform fear to love, hate to compassion, nervousness to balance, anger to forgiveness, and doubt to faith, you are succeeding in escaping the darkness of Plato's 'cave' and accomplishing your Neshamas' wish. Laila channeled to us: "Life was not meant to be revealed, but to be created." Do you have the courage to find that out?

> *"Acknowledging the Mahut of life is power. Acknowledging the Mahut of life is experiencing self-love and love of Elohim—love that is imperishable, love that is all mighty, and when love is the source of things, balance is not interrupted."*
> **El Elinos, via Laila Barzeski.**

As we have reached the end of the book; I would like to thank you all for coming on this journey. If you would like to offer your support, then the best way to do so would be to leave us your 5-star reviews and share this book with those you think it will help.

References

- Abraham hicks works https://www.abraham-hicks.com/

- Ben Ha'Elohim, Channeler of supreme guidance, Laila Barzeski - https://www.lailabr.com/

- Plato. Rouse, W.H.D. (ed.). The Republic Book VII. Penguin Group Inc. pp. 365–401.

- Schneider, Maya. From science to Consciousness, Ophir Bikkurim, 2018.

- The children of the law of One & The lost teachings of Atlantis, Network, 1997.

What is 'Hibur le Muda'ut Al' all about?

'Hibur le Muda'ut Al' was received via channeling by Laila Barzeski, Ben Ha'Elohim. The Tokhna brings frequencies, tool sets, and primary knowledge to help humanity bring more balance and ease to their life. The frequencies of the Tokhna balance and clear energy blocks in the physical body and ease on pain and even illness.

As humanity as a whole didn't succeed in making breakthroughs and is still stuck in difficulties of the material world, the purpose of the Meydai'm is to bring understanding and efficient, pragmatic tools that greatly and quickly balance the soul-spirit-mind-body connection. By opening a channel to the Inner Being, the students are able to bring forward their innate abilities to change and enhance their life.

'Hibur le Muda'ut Al' is a step-by-step program that handles a specific topic and provides knowledge and energy healing tools to resolve it.

At the teaching session, the guide charges the student, and they listen together to the frequency of the specific entry. Without charging and hearing the frequency, the energy healing tools can't be contained and applied by the student.

About the Author

Dr. Dalia Olshvang is a spiritual mentor and healer who has spent many years unraveling the secrets of personal human change and how to optimize Problem Solving Processes. Via 'Hibur le Muda'ut Al,' a step-by-step system that is unique in its depth and effectiveness, Dr. Olshvang guides people towards becoming self-empowered beings that create their reality, understand the How and the Why of their journey while unlocking the big questions of their lives. Dr. Olshvang holds a Philosophy degree from the Hebrew University of Jerusalem. She is a mom, a business leader, and a living example of everything she teaches.

Photo by: Tal Reichert

The Art of Self Value – start the journey

Go beyond the book – continue your journey and enrich your experience with additional teachings by Dalia Olshvang. Visit:

www.soulawakeningco.com

Copyright © 2022 by Dalia Olshvang
All rights reserved.

www.ingramcontent.com/pod-product-compliance
Lightning Source LLC
Chambersburg PA
CBHW042049290426
44109CB00006B/157